*2013 Case Supplement*

# Constitutional Law: Cases in Context,
**Second Edition**

# Constitutional Rights: Cases in Context

# Constitutional Structure: Cases in Context

# EDITORIAL ADVISORS

2013 Case Supplement

# Constitutional Law: Cases in Context, Second Edition

# Constitutional Rights: Cases in Context

# Constitutional Structure: Cases in Context

**Randy E. Barnett**
*Carmack Waterhouse Professor of Legal Theory*
*Georgetown University Law Center*

Wolters Kluwer
Law & Business

Published by Wolters Kluwer Law & Business in New York.

Wolters Kluwer Law & Business serves customers worldwide with CCH, Aspen Publishers, and Kluwer Law International products. (www.wolterskluwerlb.com)



To contact Customer Service, e-mail customer.service@wolterskluwer.com, call 1-800-234-1660, fax 1-800-901-9075, or mail correspondence to:

Wolters Kluwer Law & Business
Attn: Order Department
PO Box 990
Frederick, MD 21705

Printed in the United States of America.

1 2 3 4 5 6 7 8 9 0

ISBN 978-1-4548-2822-8

# About Wolters Kluwer Law & Business

Wolters Kluwer Law & Business is a leading global provider of intelligent information and digital solutions for legal and business professionals in key specialty areas, and respected educational resources for professors and law students. Wolters Kluwer Law & Business connects legal and business professionals as well as those in the education market with timely, specialized authoritative content and information-enabled solutions to support success through productivity, accuracy and mobility.

Serving customers worldwide, Wolters Kluwer Law & Business products include those under the Aspen Publishers, CCH, Kluwer Law International, Loislaw, ftwilliam.com and MediRegs family of products.

**CCH** products have been a trusted resource since 1913, and are highly regarded resources for legal, securities, antitrust and trade regulation, government contracting, banking, pension, payroll, employment and labor, and healthcare reimbursement and compliance professionals.

**Aspen Publishers** products provide essential information to attorneys, business professionals and law students. Written by preeminent authorities, the product line offers analytical and practical information in a range of specialty practice areas from securities law and intellectual property to mergers and acquisitions and pension/benefits. Aspen's trusted legal education resources provide professors and students with high-quality, up-to-date and effective resources for successful instruction and study in all areas of the law.

**Kluwer Law International** products provide the global business community with reliable international legal information in English. Legal practitioners, corporate counsel and business executives around the world rely on Kluwer Law journals, looseleafs, books, and electronic products for comprehensive information in many areas of international legal practice.

**Loislaw** is a comprehensive online legal research product providing legal content to law firm practitioners of various specializations. Loislaw provides attorneys with the ability to quickly and efficiently find the necessary legal information they need, when and where they need it, by facilitating access to primary law as well as state-specific law, records, forms and treatises.

**ftwilliam.com** offers employee benefits professionals the highest quality plan documents (retirement, welfare and non-qualified) and government forms (5500/PBGC, 1099 and IRS) software at highly competitive prices.

**MediRegs** products provide integrated health care compliance content and software solutions for professionals in healthcare, higher education and life sciences, including professionals in accounting, law and consulting.

Wolters Kluwer Law & Business, a division of Wolters Kluwer, is headquartered in New York. Wolters Kluwer is a market-leading global information services company focused on professionals.

# Contents

*2013 Case Supplement*

# Constitutional Law: Cases in Context,
**Second Edition**

# Constitutional Rights: Cases in Context

# Constitutional Structure: Cases in Context

# Chapter 1

# The Founding: Further Readings on the Origins of the Constitution

## ASSIGNMENT S-1

### 1. John Locke: On the State of Nature and the Origin and Purpose of Civil Society and Government

The Founders were very much influenced by such natural rights thinkers as John Locke, Hugo Grotious, Samuel von Pufendorf, and Emmerich de Vattel. What follows is the fuller passages from which the excerpts appearing the casebook were taken.

***Study Guide:***

- What do you suppose is the persistent appeal of "state of nature" theorizing?
- How does Locke's vision of the "state of nature" differ from that of Hobbes (as it appears in the casebook)?
- Can you imagine why these words of Locke would be considered so great a threat to the established authority in general and of the Crown in particular?
- What is Locke's argument for government?
- What does he say is lacking in the state of nature?
- What is his argument for majority rule?
- Can a majority form a government over a dissenting minority?
- Finally, notice how Locke identifies the separation of legislative, executive, and judicial powers.

## JOHN LOCKE, SECOND TREATISE OF GOVERNMENT: AN ESSAY CONCERNING THE TRUE ORIGINAL, EXTENT AND END OF CIVIL GOVERNMENT, 1690

### CHAPTER 2
### *Of the State of Nature*

§4. To understand political power right, and derive it from its original, we must consider, what state all men are naturally in, and that is, a state of perfect freedom to order their actions, and dispose of their possessions and persons, as they think fit, within the bounds of the law of nature, without asking leave, or depending upon the will of any other man.

A state also of equality, wherein all the power and jurisdiction is reciprocal, no one having more than another; there being nothing more evident, than that creatures of the same species and rank, promiscuously born to all the same advantages of nature, and the use of the same faculties, should also be equal one amongst another without subordination or subjection, unless the lord and master of them all should, by any manifest declaration of his will, set one above another, and confer on him, by an evident and clear appointment, an undoubted right to dominion and sovereignty. . . .

§6. But though this be a state of liberty, yet it is not a state of licence: though man in that state have an uncontroulable liberty to dispose of his person or possessions, yet he has not liberty to destroy himself, or so much as any creature in his possession, but where some nobler use than its bare preservation calls for it. The state of nature has a law of nature to govern it, which obliges every one: and reason, which is that law, teaches all mankind, who will but consult it, that being all equal and independent, no one ought to harm another in his life, health, liberty, or possessions: for men being all the workmanship of one omnipotent, and infinitely wise maker; all the servants of one sovereign master, sent into the world by his order, and about his business; they are his property, whose workmanship they are, made to last during his, not one another's pleasure: and being furnished with like faculties, sharing all in one community of nature, there cannot be supposed any such subordination among us, that may authorize us to destroy one another, as if we were made for one another's uses, as the inferior ranks of creatures are for ours. Every one, as he is bound to preserve himself, and not to quit his station wilfully, so by the like reason, when his own preservation comes not in competition, ought he, as much as he can, to preserve the rest of mankind, and may not, unless it be to do justice on an offender, take away, or impair the life, or what tends to the preservation of the life, the liberty, health, limb, or goods of another.

§7. And that all men may be restrained from invading others' rights, and from doing hurt to one another, and the law of nature be observed, which willeth the peace and preservation of all mankind, the execution of the law of nature is, in that state, put into every man's hands, whereby every one has a right to punish the transgressors of that law to such a degree, as may hinder its violation: for the law of nature would, as all other laws that concern men in this world be in vain, if there were no body that in the state of nature had a power to execute that law, and thereby preserve the innocent and restrain offenders. And if any one in the state of nature may punish another for any evil he has done, every one may do so: for in that state of perfect equality, where naturally there is no superiority or jurisdiction of one over another, what any may do in prosecution of that law, every one must needs have a right to do.

§8. And thus, in the state of nature, one man comes by a power over another; but yet no absolute or arbitrary power, to use a criminal, when he has got him in his hands, according to the passionate heats, or boundless extravagancy of his own will; but only to retribute to him, so far as calm reason and conscience dictate, what is proportionate to his transgression, which is so much as may serve for reparation and restraint: for these two are the only reasons, why one man may lawfully do harm to another, which is that we call punishment. In transgressing the law of nature, the offender declares himself to live by another rule than that of reason and common equity, which is that measure God has set to the actions of men, for their mutual security; and so he becomes dangerous to mankind, the tye, which is to secure them from injury and violence, being slighted and broken by him. Which being a trespass against the whole species, and the peace and safety of it, provided for by the law of nature, every man upon this score, by the right he hath to preserve mankind in general, may restrain, or where it is necessary, destroy things noxious to them, and so may bring such evil on any one, who hath transgressed that law, as may make him repent the doing of it, and thereby deter him, and by his example others, from doing the like mischief. And in the case, and upon this ground, EVERY MAN HATH A RIGHT TO PUNISH THE OFFENDER, AND BE EXECUTIONER OF THE LAW OF NATURE. . . .

§11. From these two distinct rights, the one of punishing the crime for restraint, and preventing the like offence, which right of punishing is in every body; the other of taking reparation, which belongs only to the injured party, comes it to pass that the magistrate, who by being magistrate hath the common right of punishing put into his hands, can often, where the public good demands not the execution of the law, remit the punishment of criminal offences by his own authority, but yet cannot remit the satisfaction due to any private man for the damage he has received. That, he who has suffered the damage has a right to demand in his own name. . . .

§13. To this strange doctrine, viz. That in the state of nature every one has the executive power of the law of nature, I doubt not but it will be objected, that it is unreasonable for men to be judges in their own cases, that self-love will make men partial to themselves and their friends: and on the other side, that ill nature, passion and revenge will carry them too far in punishing others; and hence nothing but confusion and disorder will follow, and that therefore God hath certainly appointed government to restrain the partiality and violence of men. I easily grant, that civil government is the proper remedy for the inconveniencies of the state of nature, which must certainly be great, where men may be judges in their own case, since it is easy to be imagined, that he who was so unjust as to do his brother an injury, will scarce be so just as to condemn himself for it: but I shall desire those who make this objection, to remember, that absolute monarchs are but men; and if government is to be the remedy of those evils, which necessarily follow from men's being judges in their own cases, and the state of nature is therefore not to be endured, I desire to know what kind of government that is, and how much better it is than the state of nature, where one man, commanding a multitude, has the liberty to be judge in his own case, and may do to all his subjects whatever he pleases, without the least liberty to any one to question or controul those who execute his pleasure and in whatsoever he doth, whether led by reason, mistake or passion, must be submitted to. Much better it is in the state of nature, wherein men are not bound to submit to the unjust will of another. And if he that judges, judges amiss in his own, or any other case, he is answerable for it to the rest of mankind.

§14. It is often asked as a mighty objection, where are, or ever were there any men in such a state of nature? To which it may suffice as an answer at present, that since all princes and rulers of independent governments all through the world, are in a state of nature, it is plain the world never was, nor ever will be, without numbers of men in that state. I have named all governors of independent communities, whether they are, or are not, in league with others: for it is not every compact that puts an end to the state of nature between men, but only this one of agreeing together mutually to enter into one community, and make one body politic; other promises, and compacts, men may make one with another, and yet still be in the state of nature. The promises and bargains for truck, &c. between the two men in the desert island, mentioned by Garcilasso de la Vega, in his history of Peru; or between a Swiss and an Indian, in the woods of America, are binding to them, though they are perfectly in a state of nature, in reference to one another: for truth and keeping of faith belongs to men, as men, and not as members of society. . . .

## CHAPTER 8
### *Of the Beginning of Political Societies*

§95. Men being, as has been said, by nature, all free, equal, and independent, no one can be put out of this estate, and subjected to the political power of another, without his own consent. The only way whereby any one divests himself of his natural liberty, and puts on the bonds of civil society, is by agreeing with other men to join and unite into a community for their comfortable, safe, and peaceable living one amongst another, in a secure enjoyment of their properties, and a greater security against any, that are not of it. This any number of men may do, because it injures not the freedom of the rest; they are left as they were in the liberty of the state of nature. When any number of men have so consented to make one community or government, they are thereby presently incorporated, and make one body politic, wherein the majority have a right to act and conclude the rest.

§96. For when any number of men have, by the consent of every individual, made a community, they have thereby made that community one body, with a power to act as one body, which is only by the will and determination of the majority: for that which acts any community, being only the consent of the individuals of it, and it being necessary to that which is one body to move one way; it is necessary the body should move that way whither the greater force carries it, which is the consent of the majority: . . . and so every one is bound by that consent to be concluded by the majority. . . .

§97. And thus every man, by consenting with others to make one body politic under one government, puts himself under an obligation, to every one of that society, to submit to the determination of the majority, and to be concluded by it; or else this original compact, whereby he with others incorporates into one society, would signify nothing, and be no compact, if he be left free, and under no other ties than he was in before in the state of nature. . . .

§98. For if the consent of the majority shall not, in reason, be received as the act of the whole, and conclude every individual; nothing but the consent of every individual can make any thing to be the act of the whole: but such a consent is next to impossible ever to be had, if we consider the infirmities of health, and avocations of business, which in a number, though much less than that of a commonwealth, will necessarily keep many away from the public assembly. To which if we add the variety of opinions, and contrariety of interests, . . . [s]uch a constitution as this would make the mighty Leviathan of a shorter duration, than the feeblest creatures, and not let it outlast the day it was born. . . .

§99. Whosoever therefore out of a state of nature unite into a community, must be understood to give up all the power, necessary to the ends for which they unite into society, to the majority of the community, unless they expressly agreed in any number greater than the majority. And this is done by barely agreeing to unite into one political society, which is all the compact that is, or needs be, between the individuals, that enter into, or make up a commonwealth. And thus that, which begins and actually constitutes any political society, is nothing but the consent of any number of freemen capable of a majority to unite and incorporate into such a society. And this is that, and that only, which did, or could give beginning to any lawful government in the world. . . .

## CHAPTER 9
### *Of the Ends of Political Society and Government*

§123. If man in the state of nature be so free, as has been said; if he be absolute lord of his own person and possessions, equal to the greatest, and subject to no body, why will he part with his freedom? Why will he give up this empire, and subject himself to the dominion and controul of any other power? To which it is obvious to answer, that though in the state of nature he hath such a right, yet the enjoyment of it is very uncertain, and constantly exposed to the invasion of others: for all being kings as much as he, every man his equal, and the greater part no strict observers of equity and justice, the enjoyment of the property he has in this state is very unsafe, very unsecure. This makes him willing to quit a condition, which, however free, is full of fears and continual dangers: and it is not without reason, that he seeks out, and is willing to join in society with others, who are already united, or have a mind to unite, for the mutual preservation of their lives, liberties and estates, which I call by the general name, property.

§124. The great and chief end, therefore, of men's uniting into commonwealths, and putting themselves under government, is the preservation of their property. To which in the state of nature there are many things wanting.

First, There wants an established, settled, known law, received and allowed by common consent to be the standard of right and wrong, and the common measure to decide all controversies between them: for though the law of nature be plain and intelligible to all rational creatures; yet men being biassed by their interest, as well as ignorant for want of study of it, are not apt to allow of it as a law binding to them in the application of it to their particular cases.

§125. Secondly, In the state of nature there wants a known and indifferent judge, with authority to determine all differences according to the established law: for every one in that state being both judge and executioner of the law of nature, men being partial to themselves, passion and revenge is very apt to carry them too far, and with too much heat, in their own cases; as well as negligence, and unconcernedness, to make them too remiss in other men's.

§126. Thirdly, In the state of nature there often wants power to back and support the sentence when right, and to give it due execution, They who by any injustice offended, will seldom fail, where they are able, by force to make good their injustice; such resistance many times makes the punishment dangerous, and frequently destructive, to those who attempt it.

§127. Thus mankind, notwithstanding all the privileges of the state of nature, being but in an ill condition, while they remain in it, are quickly driven into society. Hence it comes to pass, that we seldom find any number of men live any time together in this state. The inconveniencies that they are therein exposed to, by the irregular and uncertain exercise of the power every man has of punishing the transgressions of others, make them take sanctuary under the established laws of government, and therein seek the preservation of their property. It is this makes them so willingly give up every one his single power of punishing, to be exercised by such alone, as shall be appointed to it amongst them; and by such rules as the community, or those authorized by them to that purpose, shall agree on. And in this we have the original right and rise of both the legislative and executive power, as well as of the governments and societies themselves.

§128. For in the state of nature, to omit the liberty he has of innocent delights, a man has two powers.

The first is to do whatsoever he thinks fit for the preservation of himself, and others within the permission of the law of nature: by which law, common to them all, he and all the rest of mankind are one community, make up one society, distinct from all other creatures. And were it not for the corruption and vitiousness of degenerate men, there would be no need of any other; no necessity that men should separate from this great and natural community, and by positive agreements combine into smaller and divided associations.

The other power a man has in the state of nature, is the power to punish the crimes committed against that law. Both these he gives up, when he joins in a private, if I may so call it, or particular politic society, and incorporates into any common wealth, separate from the rest of mankind.

§129. The first power, viz. of doing whatsoever he thought for the preservation of himself, and the rest of mankind, he gives up to be regulated by laws made by the society, so far forth as the preservation of himself, and the rest of that society shall require; which laws of the society in many things confine the liberty he had by the law of nature.

§130. Secondly, The power of punishing he wholly gives up, and engages his natural force, (which he might before employ in the execution of the law of nature, by his own single authority, as he thought fit) to assist the executive power of the society, as the law thereof shall require: for being now in a new state, wherein he is to enjoy many conveniencies, from the labour, assistance, and society of others in the same community, as well as protection from its whole strength; he is to part also with as much of his natural liberty, in providing for himself, as the good, prosperity, and safety of the society shall require; which is not only necessary, but just, since the other members of the society do the like.

§131. But though men, when they enter into society, give up the equality, liberty, and executive power they had in the state of nature, into the hands of the society, to be so far disposed of by the legislative, as the good of the society shall require; yet it being only with an intention in every one the better to preserve himself, his liberty and property; (for no rational creature can be supposed to change his condition with an intention to be worse) the power of the society, or legislative constituted by them, can never be supposed to extend farther, than the common good; but is obliged to secure every one's property, by providing against those three defects above mentioned, that made the state of nature so unsafe and uneasy. And so whoever has the legislative or supreme power of any commonwealth, is bound to govern by established standing laws, promulgated and known to the people, and not by extemporary decrees; by indifferent and upright judges, who are to decide controversies by those laws; and to employ the force of the community at home, only in the execution of such laws, or abroad to prevent or redress foreign injuries, and secure the community from inroads and invasion. And all this to be directed to no other end, but the peace, safety, and public good of the people.

## *ASSIGNMENT S-2*

## 2. James Madison: On the Alleged Failure of the Articles of Confederation

Prior to the adoption of the Constitution, the United States was governed by the Articles of Confederation (which appear in the beginning of the casebook). During the post-Revolutionary period, many Americans became unhappy with the general state of the economy and with the behavior of state governments. In an essay prepared in advance of the Philadelphia convention, Madison summarized what he and others perceived as the deficiencies or "vices" in the form of government defined by the Articles. That the Articles were deficient in these ways was one of the principal assumptions underlying the formulation and eventual adoption of the Constitution. The list he provided is a useful summary of these defenses.

Madison also addresses an important problem with then-prevalent political theory: how to explain the adoption of bad policies and widespread violations of rights by state governments that are "republican" in form and therefore accountable to "the People." At the time, state governments were largely run by a single popularly elected assembly, to which the executive and judiciary were subservient. Such governments were widely thought to be the proper alternative to rule by an aristocracy as the means of protecting the retained rights of the people. Yet, those who favored a new constitutional structure believed these republican governments to be pervasively violating the people's rights, which was simply not supposed to happen.

In this essay (summarized by bullet points in the casebook), Madison attempts to answer this question with an early version of the argument he later presents in *The Federalist, No. 10*: his theory of "faction" that explains how majoritarian rule can come to violate unjustly the rights of the people.

***Study Guide:***

- When reading Madison's complaints about the Articles, you must keep in mind that a great many people either did not share these complaints, or thought that they could be cured by making changes to the Articles, rather than by replacing them altogether. For this reason, when the Constitution was proposed, it was also bitterly opposed.
- There is much of interest in this essay that presages the new Constitution, as well as future constitutional controversies. One is Madison's strong concern for commerce. Another is his belief that a constitution should be ratified by the people. Why was that deemed by him to be so important?
- What is Madison's proposed solution to the problem of faction?

**JAMES MADISON, VICES OF THE POLITICAL SYSTEM OF THE UNITED STATES, APRIL 1787:** 1. *Failure of the States to comply with the Constitutional requisitions.* This evil has been so fully experienced both during the war and since the peace, results so naturally from the number and independent authority of the States and has been so uniformly exemplified in every similar Confederacy, that it may be considered as not less radically and permanently inherent in, than it is fatal to the object of, the present System.

2. *Encroachments by the States on the federal authority.* Examples of this are numerous and repetitions may be foreseen in almost every case where any favorite object of a State shall present a temptation. Among these examples are the wars and Treaties of Georgia with the Indians—The unlicensed compacts between Virginia and Maryland, and between Pena. & N. Jersey—the troops raised and to be kept up by Massts.

3. *Violations of the law of nations and of treaties.* From the number of Legislatures, the sphere of life from which most of their members are taken, and the circumstances under which their legislative business is carried on,

irregularities of this kind must frequently happen. Accordingly not a year has passed without instances of them in some one or other of the States. The Treaty of peace—the treaty with France—the treaty with Holland have each been violated. The causes of these irregularities must necessarily produce frequent violations of the law of nations in other respects.

As yet foreign powers have not been rigorous in animadverting on us. This moderation however cannot be mistaken for a permanent partiality to our faults, or a permanent security agst. those disputes with other nations, which being among the greatest of public calamities, it ought to be least in the power of any part of the Community to bring on the whole.

4. *Trespasses of the States on the rights of each other.* These are alarming symptoms, and may be daily apprehended as we are admonished by daily experience. See the law of Virginia restricting foreign vessels to certain ports—of Maryland in favor of vessels belonging to her own citizens—of N. York in favor of the same.

Paper money, instalments of debts, occlusion of Courts, making property a legal tender, may likewise be deemed aggressions on the rights of other States. As the Citizens of every State aggregately taken stand more or less in the relation of Creditors or debtors, to the Citizens of every other States, Acts of the debtor State in favor of debtors, affect the Creditor State, in the same manner, as they do its own citizens who are relatively creditors towards other citizens. This remark may be extended to foreign nations. If the exclusive regulation of the value and alloy of coin was properly delegated to the federal authority, the policy of it equally requires a controul on the States in the cases above mentioned. It must have been meant 1. to preserve uniformity in the circulating medium throughout the nation. 2. to prevent those frauds on the citizens of other States, and the subjects of foreign powers, which might disturb the tranquility at home, or involve the Union in foreign contests.

The practice of many States in restricting the commercial intercourse with other States, and putting their productions and manufactures on the same footing with those of foreign nations, though not contrary to the federal articles, is certainly adverse to the spirit of the Union, and tends to beget retaliating regulations, not less expensive & vexatious in themselves, than they are destructive of the general harmony.

5. *Want of concert in matters where common interest requires it.* This defect is strongly illustrated in the state of our commercial affairs. How much has the national dignity, interest, and revenue suffered from this cause? Instances of inferior moment are the want of uniformity in the laws concerning naturalization & literary property; of provision for national seminaries, for grants of incorporation for national purposes, for canals and other works of general utility, wch. may at present be defeated by the perverseness of particular States whose concurrence is necessary.

6. *Want of guaranty to the States of their Constitutions & laws against internal violence.* The confederation is silent on this point and therefore by the second article the hands of the federal authority are tied. According to Republican Theory, Right and power being both vested in the majority, are held to be

synonimous. According to fact and experience a minority may in an appeal to force, be an overmatch for the majority. 1. If the minority happen to include all such as possess the skill and habits of military life, & such as possess the great pecuniary resources, one third only may conquer the remaining two thirds. 2. One third of those who participate in the choice of the rulers, may be rendered a majority by the accession of those whose poverty excludes them from a right of suffrage, and who for obvious reasons will be more likely to join the standard of sedition than that of the established Government. 3. Where slavery exists the republican Theory becomes still more fallacious.

7. *Want of sanction to the laws, and of coercion in the Government of the Confederacy.* A sanction is essential to the idea of law, as coercion is to that of Government. The federal system being destitute of both, wants the great vital principles of a Political Cons[ti]tution. Under the form of such a Constitution, it is in fact nothing more than a treaty of amity of commerce and of alliance, between so many independent and Sovereign States. From what cause could so fatal an omission have happened in the articles of Confederation? from a mistaken confidence that the justice, the good faith, the honor, the sound policy, of the several legislative assemblies would render superfluous any appeal to the ordinary motives by which the laws secure the obedience of individuals: a confidence which does honor to the enthusiastic virtue of the compilers, as much as the inexperience of the crisis apologizes for their errors. The time which has since elapsed has had the double effect, of increasing the light, and tempering the warmth, with which the arduous work may be revised. It is no longer doubted that a unanimous and punctual obedience of 13 independent bodies, to the acts of the federal Government, ought not be calculated on. Even during the war, when external danger supplied in some degree the defect of legal & coercive sanctions, how imperfectly did the States fulfil their obligations to the Union? In time of peace, we see already what is to be expected. How indeed could it be otherwise? In the first place, Every general act of the Union must necessarily bear unequally hard on some particular member or members of it. Secondly the partiality of the members to their own interests and rights, a partiality which will be fostered by the Courtiers of popularity, will naturally exaggerate the inequality where it exists, and even suspect it where it has no existence. Thirdly a distrust of the voluntary compliance of each other may prevent the compliance of any, although it should be the latent disposition of all. Here are causes & pretexts which will never fail to render federal measures abortive. If the laws of the States, were merely recommendatory to their citizens, or if they were to be rejudged by County authorities, what security, what probability would exist, that they would be carried into execution? Is the security or probability greater in favor of the acts of Congs. which depending for their execution on the will of the state legislatures, wch. are tho' nominally authoritative, in fact recommendatory only.

8. *Want of ratification by the people of the articles of Confederation.* In some of the States the Confederation is recognized by, and forms a part of the constitution. In others however it has received no other sanction than that of the Legislative authority. From this defect two evils result: 1. Whenever a law of a State happens to be repugnant to an act of Congress, particularly when the latter

is of posterior date to the former, it will be at least questionable whether the latter must not prevail; and as the question must be decided by the Tribunals of the State, they will be most likely to lean on the side of the State. 2. As far as the Union of the States is to be regarded as a league of sovereign powers, and not as a political Constitution by virtue of which they are become one sovereign power, so far it seems to follow from the doctrine of compacts, that a breach of any of the articles of the confederation by any of the parties to it, absolves the other parties from their respective obligations, and gives them a right if they chuse to exert it, of dissolving the Union altogether.

9. *Multiplicity of laws in the several States.* . . . Among the evils . . . of our situation may well be ranked the multiplicity of laws from which no State is exempt. As far as laws are necessary, to mark with precision the duties of those who are to obey them, and to take from those who are to administer them a discretion, which might be abused, their number is the price of liberty. As far as the laws exceed this limit, they are a nusance: a nusance of the most pestilent kind. Try the Codes of the several States by this test, and what a luxuriancy of legislation do they present. The short period of independency has filled as many pages as the century which preceded it. Every year, almost every session, adds a new volume. This may be the effect in part, but it can only be in part, of the situation in which the revolution has placed us. A review of the several codes will shew that every necessary and useful part of the least voluminous of them might be compressed into one tenth of the compass, and at the same time be rendered tenfold as perspicuous.

10. *Mutability of the laws of the States.* . . . We daily see laws repealed or superseded, before any trial can have been made of their merits: and even before a knowledge of them can have reached the remoter districts within which they were to operate. In the regulations of trade this instability becomes a snare not only to our citizens but to foreigners also.

11. *Injustice of the laws of States.* If the multiplicity and mutability of laws prove a want of wisdom, their injustice betrays a defect still more alarming: more alarming not merely because it is a greater evil in itself, but because it brings more into question the fundamental principle of republican Government, that the majority who rule in such Governments, are the safest Guardians both of public Good and of private rights. To what causes is this evil to be ascribed?

These causes lie 1. in the Representative bodies. 2. in the people themselves.

1. Representative appointments are sought from 3 motives. 1. ambition 2. personal interest. 3. public good. Unhappily the two first are proved by experience to be most prevalent. Hence the candidates who feel them, particularly, the second, are most industrious, and most successful in pursuing their object: and forming often a majority in the legislative Councils, with interested views, contrary to the interest, and views, of their Constituents, join in a perfidious sacrifice of the latter to the former. A succeeding election it might be supposed, would displace the offenders, and repair the mischief. But how easily are base and selfish measures, masked by pretexts of public good and apparent expediency? How frequently will a repetition of the same arts and industry which succeeded in the first instance, again prevail on the unwary to misplace their confidence?

How frequently too will the honest but unenlightened representative be the dupe of a favorite leader, veiling his selfish views under the professions of public good, and varnishing his sophistical arguments with the glowing colours of popular eloquence?

2. A still more fatal if not more frequent cause lies among the people themselves. All civilized societies are divided into different interests and factions, as they happen to be creditors or debtors—Rich or poor—husbandmen, merchants or manufacturers—members of different religious sects—followers of different political leaders—inhabitants of different districts—owners of different kinds of property &c. &c. In republican Government the majority however composed, ultimately give the law. Whenever therefore an apparent interest or common passion unites a majority what is to restrain them from unjust violations of the rights and interests of the minority, or of individuals? Three motives only:

> 1. a prudent regard to their own good as involved in the general and permanent good of the Community. This consideration although of decisive weight in itself, is found by experience to be too often unheeded. It is too often forgotten, by nations as well as by individuals that honesty is the best policy.
>
> 2dly. respect for character. However strong this motive may be in individuals, it is considered as very insufficient to restrain them from injustice. In a multitude its efficacy is diminished in proportion to the number which is to share the praise or the blame. Besides, as it has reference to public opinion, which within a particular Society, is the opinion of the majority, the standard is fixed by those whose conduct is to be measured by it. The public opinion without the Society, will be little respected by the people at large of any Country. Individuals of extended views, and of national pride, may bring the public proceedings to this standard, but the example will never be followed by the multitude. Is it to be imagined that an ordinary citizen or even an assemblyman of R. Island in estimating the policy of paper money, ever considered or cared in what light the measure would be viewed in France or Holland; or even in Massts or Connect.? It was a sufficient temptation to both that it was for their interest: it was a sufficient sanction to the latter that it was popular in the State; to the former that it was so in the neighbourhood.
>
> 3dly. will Religion the only remaining motive be a sufficient restraint? It is not pretended to be such on men individually considered. Will its effect be greater on them considered in an aggregate view? quite the reverse. The conduct of every popular assembly acting on oath, the strongest of religious Ties, proves that individuals join without remorse in acts, against which their consciences would revolt if proposed to them under the like sanction, separately in their closets. When indeed Religion is kindled into enthusiasm, its force like that of other passions, is increased by the sympathy of a multitude. But enthusiasm is only a temporary state of religion, and while it lasts will hardly be seen with pleasure at the helm of Government. Besides as religion in its coolest state, is not infallible, it may become a motive to oppression as well as a restraint from injustice.

Place three individuals in a situation wherein the interest of each depends on the voice of the others, and give to two of them an interest opposed to the rights of the third? Will the latter be secure? The prudence of every man would shun the danger. The rules & forms of justice suppose & guard against it. Will two thousand in a like situation be less likely to encroach on the rights of one thousand? The contrary is witnessed by the notorious factions & oppressions which take place in corporate towns limited as the opportunities are, and in little republics when uncontrouled by apprehensions of external danger. If an enlargement of the sphere is found to lessen the insecurity of private rights, it is not because the impulse of a common interest or passion is less predominant in this case with the majority; but because a common interest or passion is less apt to be felt and the requisite combinations less easy to be formed by a great than by a small number. The Society becomes broken into a greater variety of interests, of pursuits, of passions, which check each other, whilst those who may feel a common sentiment have less opportunity of communication and concert. It may be inferred that the inconveniences of popular States contrary to the prevailing Theory, are in proportion not to the extent, but to the narrowness of their limits.

The great desideratum in Government is such a modification of the Sovereignty as will render it sufficiently neutral between the different interests and factions, to controul one part of the Society from invading the rights of another, and at the same time sufficiently controuled itself, from setting up an interest adverse to that of the whole Society. In absolute Monarchies, the prince is sufficiently, neutral towards his subjects, but frequently sacrifices their happiness to his ambition or his avarice. In small Republics, the sovereign will is sufficiently controuled from such a Sacrifice of the entire Society, but is not sufficiently neutral towards the parts composing it. As a limited Monarchy tempers the evils of an absolute one; so an extensive Republic meliorates the administration of a small Republic.

An auxiliary desideratum for the melioration of the Republican form is such a process of elections as will most certainly extract from the mass of the Society the purest and noblest characters which it contains; such as will at once feel most strongly the proper motives to pursue the end of their appointment, and be most capable to devise the proper means of attaining it.

# *Chapter 2*

# *Enumerated Powers*

## *ASSIGNMENT S-3*

### The Roberts Court

### The Commerce and Necessary and Proper Clauses

*Study Guide:*

- The next case is noteworthy, not for its majority opinion that is based on statutory interpretation, but for the concurring opinion by Justice Thomas in which he discusses the scope of the Indian Commerce Clause.
- Some scholars have contended that, because the first statute regulating "intercourse" with Indian tribes reflected a broader meaning of "commerce" than Justice Thomas attributed to the Interstate Commerce Clause, his interpretation of "commerce" is refuted.
- What follows is a brief point-counterpoint by Jack Balkin and Robert Natelson discussing the 1790 statute.

### ADOPTIVE COUPLE v. BABY GIRL

*No. 12-399. | Decided June 25, 2013*

Justice Alito delivered the opinion of the Court.

This case is about a little girl (Baby Girl) who is classified as an Indian because she is 1.2% (3/256) Cherokee. Because Baby Girl is classified in this way, the South Carolina Supreme Court held that certain provisions of the federal Indian Child Welfare Act of 1978 required her to be taken, at the age of 27 months, from the only parents she had ever known and handed over to her biological father, who had attempted to relinquish his parental rights and who had no prior contact with the child. The provisions of the federal statute at issue here do not demand this result. Contrary to the State Supreme Court's ruling, we hold that 25 U.S.C. §1912(f)—which bars involuntary termination of a parent's rights in the absence of a heightened showing that serious harm to the Indian child is likely to result from the parent's "continued custody" of the child—does not apply when, as here, the relevant parent never had custody of the child. We further hold that §1912(d)—which conditions involuntary termination of parental rights with respect to an Indian child on a showing that remedial efforts have been made to prevent the "breakup of the Indian family"—is inapplicable when, as here, the parent abandoned the Indian child before birth and never had custody of the child. Finally, we clarify that §1915(a), which provides placement preferences for the adoption of Indian children, does not bar a non-Indian family like Adoptive Couple from adopting an Indian child when no other eligible candidates have sought to adopt the child. We accordingly reverse the South Carolina Supreme Court's judgment and remand for further proceedings. . . .

The Indian Child Welfare Act was enacted to help preserve the cultural identity and heritage of Indian tribes, but under the State Supreme Court's reading, the Act would put certain vulnerable children at a great disadvantage solely because an ancestor—even a remote one—was an Indian. As the State Supreme Court read §§1912(d) and (f), a biological Indian father could abandon his child *in utero* and refuse any support for the birth mother—perhaps contributing to the mother's decision to put the child up for adoption—and then could play his ICWA trump card at the eleventh hour to override the mother's decision and the child's best interests. If this were possible, many prospective adoptive parents would surely pause before adopting any child who might possibly qualify as an Indian under the ICWA. Such an interpretation would raise equal protection concerns, but the plain text of §§1912(f) and (d) makes clear that neither provision applies in the present context. Nor do §1915(a)'s rebuttable adoption preferences apply when no alternative party has formally sought to adopt the child. We therefore reverse the judgment of the South Carolina Supreme Court and remand the case for further proceedings not inconsistent with this opinion.

*It is so ordered.*

JUSTICE THOMAS, concurring.

I join the Court's opinion in full but write separately to explain why constitutional avoidance compels this outcome. Each party in this case has put forward a plausible interpretation of the relevant sections of the Indian Child Welfare Act (ICWA). However, the interpretations offered by respondent Birth Father and the United States raise significant constitutional problems as applied to this case. Because the Court's decision avoids those problems, I concur in its interpretation.

I

This case arises out of a contested state-court adoption proceeding. Adoption proceedings are adjudicated in state family courts across the country every day, and "domestic relations" is "an area that has long been regarded as a virtually exclusive province of the States." *Sosna v. Iowa* (1975). Indeed, "[t]he whole subject of the domestic relations of husband and wife, parent and child, belongs to the laws of the States and not to the laws of the United States." *In re Burrus* (1890). Nevertheless, when Adoptive Couple filed a petition in South Carolina Family Court to finalize their adoption of Baby Girl, Birth Father, who had relinquished his parental rights via a text message to Birth Mother, claimed a federal right under the ICWA to block the adoption and to obtain custody.

The ICWA establishes "federal standards that govern state-court child custody proceedings involving Indian children." The ICWA defines "Indian child" as "any unmarried person who is under age eighteen and is either (a) a member of an Indian tribe or (b) is eligible for membership in an Indian tribe and is the biological child of a member of an Indian tribe." As relevant, the ICWA defines "child custody proceeding," §1903(1), to include "adoptive placement," which means "the permanent placement of an Indian child for adoption, including any action resulting in a final decree of adoption," §1903(1)(iv), and "termination of parental rights," which means "any action resulting in the termination of the parent-child relationship," §1903(1)(ii).

The ICWA restricts a state court's ability to terminate the parental rights of an Indian parent in two relevant ways. Section 1912(f) prohibits a state court from involuntarily terminating parental rights "in the absence of a determination, supported by evidence beyond a reasonable doubt, including testimony of qualified expert witnesses, that the continued custody of the child by the parent or Indian custodian is likely to result in serious emotional or physical damage to the child." Section 1912(d) prohibits a state court from terminating parental rights until the court is satisfied "that active efforts have been made to provide remedial services and rehabilitative programs designed to prevent the breakup of the Indian family and that these efforts have proved unsuccessful." A third provision creates specific placement preferences for the adoption of Indian children, which favor placement with Indians over other adoptive families. §1915(a). Operating together, these requirements often lead to different outcomes than would result under state law. That is precisely what happened here. See *ante* ("It is undisputed that, had Baby Girl not been 3/256 Cherokee, Biological Father would have had no right to object to her adoption under South Carolina law").

The ICWA recognizes States' inherent "jurisdiction over Indian child custody proceedings," §1901(5), but asserts that federal regulation is necessary because States "have often failed to recognize the essential tribal relations of Indian people and the cultural and social standards prevailing in Indian communities and families." However, Congress may regulate areas of traditional state concern only if the Constitution grants it such power. Admt. 10 ("The powers not delegated to the United States by the Constitution, nor prohibited by it to the States, are reserved to the States respectively, or to the people"). The threshold question, then, is whether the Constitution grants Congress power to override state custody law whenever an Indian is involved.

## II

The ICWA asserts that the Indian Commerce Clause, Art. I, §8, cl. 3, and "other constitutional authority" provides Congress with "plenary power over

Indian affairs." §1901(1). The reference to "other constitutional authority" is not illuminating, and I am aware of no other enumerated power that could even arguably support Congress' intrusion into this area of traditional state authority. See Fletcher, The Supreme Court and Federal Indian Policy, 85 Neb. L. Rev. 121, 137 (2006) ("As a matter of federal constitutional law, the Indian Commerce Clause grants Congress the only explicit constitutional authority to deal with Indian tribes"); Natelson, The Original Understanding of the Indian Commerce Clause, 85 Denver U. L. Rev. 201, 210 (2007) (hereinafter Natelson) (evaluating, and rejecting, other potential sources of authority supporting congressional power over Indians). The assertion of plenary authority must, therefore, stand or fall on Congress' power under the Indian Commerce Clause. Although this Court has said that the "central function of the Indian Commerce Clause is to provide Congress with plenary power to legislate in the field of Indian affairs," *Cotton Petroleum Corp. v. New Mexico* (1989), neither the text nor the original understanding of the Clause supports Congress' claim to such "plenary" power.

A

The Indian Commerce Clause gives Congress authority "[t]o regulate *Commerce* . . . with the Indian tribes." Art. I, §8, cl. 3 (emphasis added). "At the time the original Constitution was ratified, 'commerce' consisted of selling, buying, and bartering, as well as transporting for these purposes." *United States v. Lopez* (1995) (Thomas, J., concurring). See also 1 S. Johnson, A Dictionary of the English Language 361 (4th rev. ed. 1773) (reprint 1978) (defining commerce as "Intercourse; exchange of one thing for another; interchange of any thing; trade; traffick"). "[W]hen Federalists and Anti-Federalists discussed the Commerce Clause during the ratification period, they often used trade (in its selling/bartering sense) and commerce interchangeably." *Lopez* (Thomas, J., concurring). The term "commerce" did not include economic activity such as "manufacturing and agriculture," let alone noneconomic activity such as adoption of children.

Furthermore, the term "commerce with Indian tribes" was invariably used during the time of the founding to mean " 'trade with Indians.' " See, *e.g.*, Natelson (citing 18th-century sources); Report of Committee on Indian Affairs (Feb. 20, 1787), in 32 Journals of the Continental Congress 1774-1789 (R. Hill ed. 1936) (hereinafter J. Cont'l Cong.) (using the phrase "commerce with the Indians" to mean trade with the Indians). And regulation of Indian commerce generally referred to legal structures governing "the conduct of the merchants engaged in the Indian trade, the nature of the goods they sold, the prices charged, and similar matters." Natelson.

The Indian Commerce Clause contains an additional textual limitation relevant to this case: Congress is given the power to regulate Commerce "with the Indian *tribes*." The Clause does not give Congress the power to regulate commerce with all Indian *persons* any more than the Foreign Commerce Clause gives Congress the power to regulate commerce with all foreign nationals traveling within the

United States. A straightforward reading of the text, thus, confirms that Congress may only regulate commercial interactions—"commerce"—taking place with established Indian communities—"tribes." That power is far from "plenary."

B

Congress' assertion of "plenary power" over Indian affairs is also inconsistent with the history of the Indian Commerce Clause. At the time of the founding, the Clause was understood to reserve to the States general police powers with respect to Indians who were citizens of the several States. The Clause instead conferred on Congress the much narrower power to regulate trade with Indian tribes—that is, Indians who had not been incorporated into the body-politic of any State.

1

Before the Revolution, most Colonies adopted their own regulations governing Indian trade. See Natelson (citing colonial laws). Such regulations were necessary because colonial traders all too often abused their Indian trading partners, through fraud, exorbitant prices, extortion, and physical invasion of Indian territory, among other things. See 1 F. Prucha, The Great Father (1984) (hereinafter Prucha). These abuses sometimes provoked violent Indian retaliation. To mitigate these conflicts, most Colonies extensively regulated traders engaged in commerce with Indian tribes. See *e.g.*, Ordinance to Regulate Indian Affairs, Statutes of South Carolina (Aug. 31, 1751), in 16 Early American Indian Documents: Treaties and Laws, 1607-1789 (A. Vaughan and D. Rosen eds. 1998).[1] Over time, commercial regulation at the colonial level proved largely ineffective, in part because "[t]here was no uniformity among the colonies, no two sets of like regulations." Prucha.

Recognizing the need for uniform regulation of trade with the Indians, Benjamin Franklin proposed his own "articles of confederation" to the Continental Congress on July 21, 1775, which reflected his view that central control over Indian affairs should predominate over local control. 2 J. Cont'l Cong. (W. Ford ed. 1905). Franklin's proposal was not enacted, but in November 1775, Congress empowered a committee to draft regulations for the Indian trade. On July 12, 1776, the committee submitted a draft of the Articles of Confederation to Congress, which incorporated many of Franklin's proposals. The draft prohibited States from waging offensive war against the Indians without congressional authorization and granted Congress the exclusive power to acquire land from the

1. South Carolina, for example, required traders to be licensed, to be of good moral character, and to post a bond. Ordinance to Regulate Indian Affairs. A potential applicant's name was posted publicly before issuing the license, so anyone with objections had an opportunity to raise them. Restrictions were placed on employing agents and names of potential agents had to be disclosed. Traders who violated these rules were subject to substantial penalties.

Indians outside state boundaries, once those boundaries had been established. This version also gave Congress "the sole and exclusive Right and Power of . . . Regulating the Trade, and managing all Affairs with the Indians."

On August 20, 1776, the Committee of the Whole presented to Congress a revised draft, which provided Congress with "the sole and exclusive right and power of . . . regulating the trade, and managing all affairs with the Indians." Some delegates feared that the Articles gave Congress excessive power to interfere with States' jurisdiction over affairs with Indians residing within state boundaries. After further deliberation, the final result was a clause that included a broad grant of congressional authority with two significant exceptions: "The United States in Congress assembled shall also have the sole and exclusive right and power of . . . regulating the trade and managing all affairs with the Indians, not members of any of the States, provided that the legislative right of any State within its own limits be not infringed or violated." Articles of Confederation, Art. IX, cl. 4. As a result, Congress retained exclusive jurisdiction over Indian affairs outside the borders of the States; the States retained exclusive jurisdiction over relations with Member-Indians;[2] and Congress and the States "exercise[d] concurrent jurisdiction over transactions with tribal Indians within state boundaries, but congressional decisions would have to be in compliance with local law." Natelson 230. The drafting of the Articles of Confederation reveals the delegates' concern with protecting the power of the States to regulate Indian persons who were politically incorporated into the States. This concern for state power reemerged during the drafting of the Constitution.

2

The drafting history of the Constitutional Convention also supports a limited construction of the Indian Commerce Clause. On July 24, 1787, the convention elected a drafting committee—the Committee of Detail—and charged it to "report a Constitution conformable to the Resolutions passed by the Convention." 2 Records of the Federal Convention of 1787 (M. Farrand rev. 1966) (J. Madison). During the Committee's deliberations, John Rutledge, the chairman, suggested incorporating an Indian affairs power into the Constitution. The first draft reported back to the convention, however, provided Congress with authority "[t]o regulate commerce with foreign nations, and among the several States," *id.* (Madison) (Aug. 6, 1787), but did not include any specific Indian affairs clause. On August 18, James Madison proposed that the Federal Government be granted several additional powers, including the power "[t]o regulate *affairs* with the Indians as well within as without the limits of the U. States." *Id.* (J. Madison) (emphasis added). On August 22, Rutledge delivered

2. Although Indians were generally considered "members" of a State if they paid taxes or were citizens, see Natelson, the precise definition of the term was "not yet settled" at the time of the founding and was "a question of frequent perplexity and contention in the federal councils," The Federalist No. 42 (J. Madison).

the Committee of Detail's second report, which modified Madison's proposed clause. The Committee proposed to add to Congress' power "[t]o regulate commerce with foreign nations, and among the several States" the words, "and with Indians, within the Limits of any State, not subject to the laws thereof." The Committee's version, which echoed the Articles of Confederation, was far narrower than Madison's proposal. On August 31, the revised draft was submitted to a Committee of Eleven for further action. That Committee recommended adding to the Commerce Clause the phrase, "and with the Indian tribes," which the Convention ultimately adopted.

It is, thus, clear that the Framers of the Constitution were alert to the difference between the power to regulate trade with the Indians and the power to regulate all Indian affairs. By limiting Congress' power to the former, the Framers declined to grant Congress the same broad powers over Indian affairs conferred by the Articles of Confederation. See Prakash, Against Tribal Fungibility, 89 Cornell L. Rev. 1069, 1090 (2004).

During the ratification debates, opposition to the Indian Commerce Clause was nearly nonexistent. See Natelson (noting that Robert Yates, a New York Anti-Federalist was "almost the only writer who objected to any part [of] of the Commerce Clause—a clear indication that its scope was understood to be fairly narrow"). Given the Anti-Federalists' vehement opposition to the Constitution's other grants of power to the Federal Government, this silence is revealing. The ratifiers almost certainly understood the Clause to confer a relatively modest power on Congress—namely, the power to regulate trade with Indian tribes living beyond state borders. And this feature of the Constitution was welcomed by Federalists and Anti-Federalists alike due to the considerable interest in expanding trade with such Indian tribes. See, *e.g.,* The Federalist No. 42 (J. Madison) (praising the Constitution for removing the obstacles that had existed under the Articles of Confederation to federal control over "*trade* with Indians" (emphasis added)); 3 J. Elliot, The Debates in the Several State Conventions on the Adoption of the Federal Constitution 580 (2d ed. 1863) (Adam Stephens, at the Virginia ratifying convention, June 23, 1788, describing the Indian tribes residing near the Mississippi and "the variety of articles which might be obtained to advantage by trading with these people"); The Federalist No. 24 (A. Hamilton) (arguing that frontier garrisons would "be keys to the trade with the Indian nations"); Brutus (Letter) X, N.Y. J., Jan. 24, 1788 (conceding that there must be a standing army for some purposes, including "trade with Indians"). There is little evidence that the ratifiers of the Constitution understood the Indian Commerce Clause to confer anything resembling plenary power over Indian affairs. See Natelson 247-250.

### III

In light of the original understanding of the Indian Commerce Clause, the constitutional problems that would be created by application of the ICWA here are evident. First, the statute deals with "child custody proceedings," §1903(1), not "commerce." It was enacted in response to concerns that "an alarmingly high percentage of Indian families [were] broken up by the removal, often unwarranted, of their children from them by nontribal public and private agencies." §1901(4). The perceived problem was that many Indian children were "placed in non-Indian foster and adoptive homes and institutions." This problem, however, had nothing to do with commerce.

Second, the portions of the ICWA at issue here do not regulate Indian tribes as tribes. [They] apply to all child custody proceedings involving an Indian child, regardless of whether an Indian tribe is involved. This case thus does not directly implicate Congress' power to "legislate in respect to Indian *tribes*." *United States v. Lara* (2004) (emphasis added). Baby Girl was never domiciled on an Indian Reservation, and the Cherokee Nation had no jurisdiction over her. Although Birth Father is a registered member of The Cherokee Nation, he did not live on a reservation either. He was, thus, subject to the laws of the State in which he resided (Oklahoma) and of the State where his daughter resided during the custody proceedings (South Carolina). Nothing in the Indian Commerce Clause permits Congress to enact special laws applicable to Birth Father merely because of his status as an Indian.

Because adoption proceedings like this one involve neither "commerce" nor "Indian tribes," there is simply no constitutional basis for Congress' assertion of authority over such proceedings. Also, the notion that Congress can direct state courts to apply different rules of evidence and procedure merely because a person of Indian descent is involved raises absurd possibilities. Such plenary power would allow Congress to dictate specific rules of criminal procedure for state-court prosecutions against Indian defendants. Likewise, it would allow Congress to substitute federal law for state law when contract disputes involve Indians. But the Constitution does not grant Congress power to override state law whenever that law happens to be applied to Indians. Accordingly, application of the ICWA to these child custody proceedings would be unconstitutional.

* * *

Because the Court's plausible interpretation of the relevant sections of the ICWA avoids these constitutional problems, I concur.

---

**JACK M. BALKIN, COMMERCE, 109 MICH. L. REV. 1 (2010)**: Some contemporary originalists like Justice Clarence Thomas have argued that the original meaning of "commerce" is very narrow, essentially limited to the trade or exchange of goods and commodities. Thus, it would not include manufacturing, mining, or agriculture, much less any noneconomic activities. This reading is anachronistic: by focusing on the disposition of commodities it reflects a modern conception of commerce viewed as a subset of economic activity; it completely misses the eighteenth-century dimensions of commerce as a form of social intercourse. . . .

If we view the Commerce Clause through the lens of the central reasons for forming the Constitution and the central questions that faced the new nation—foreign affairs and dealings with Indian tribes—reading "commerce" to mean "intercourse" or "interactions" makes the most sense. The Clause enabled "Congress to regulate all interactions (and altercations) with foreign nations and Indian tribes," which "if improperly handled by a single state acting on its own, might lead to needless wars or compromise the interests of sister states."

One of the first things the new government did, for example, was to regulate its interactions with the Indian tribes, through a series of Trade and Intercourse Acts beginning in 1790. The title of these acts was apt: they not only required licenses for trade with Indians, but also punished "any crime upon, or trespass against, the person or property of any peaceable and friendly Indian or Indians." These crimes did not necessarily involve trade or even economic activity; they could involve assault, murder, or rape. Note as well that even if the point of regulating these crimes was because of their likely effects on trade with the Indian tribes, the activities regulated were themselves not economic. And note finally that the 1790 and 1793 Trade and Intercourse Acts could not be justified as legislation designed to enforce treaties; they applied to crimes against Indians whether or not they had signed treaties with the United States. Congress clearly believed that it could reach both economic and noneconomic activity under the Indian Commerce Clause; at the very least it believed that it could regulate non-economic activity in order to protect trade and diplomatic relations that would further trade. This is hardly surprising. It was assumed in international law at the time of the founding that international intercourse included both commercial and noncommercial aspects that were inevitably intertwined.

Neither the trade theory nor the economic theory can explain why the early Trade and Intercourse Acts would be constitutional unless we assume that Congress has the auxiliary power to regulate noneconomic (or nontrade) activity that affects foreign or Indian commerce. That is, we must assume that Congress can reach activities that do not involve trade or are not economic in order to protect its powers to regulate trade or other economic activity, perhaps under the Necessary and Proper Clause. If so, then the two theories essentially merge into the interaction theory. Note, however, that the Clause says that Congress can regulate "commerce" with foreign nations and with the Indian tribes, not "activity that affects commerce" with foreign nations and with the Indian tribes. The interaction theory is therefore more consistent with the text.

**ROBERT G. NATELSON, THE ORIGINAL UNDERSTANDING OF THE INDIAN COMMERCE CLAUSE, 85 DENV. U. L. REV. 201 (2007)**: In contending for an expansive view of the commerce power, some have argued that a portion of the Indian Intercourse Act of 1790 shows an intended meaning for Indian "commerce" that goes beyond mere trade. . . . [T]he fundamental problem with arguing that the Indian Intercourse Act sheds light on the Commerce Clause is this: the Indian Intercourse Act was not adopted pursuant to the Commerce Clause. It was adopted pursuant to the Treaty Power.

In 1785 and 1786 Congress entered into the three "Hopewell" treaties with the Cherokees, Chickasaws, and Choctaws. By the terms of all these treaties, the United States had promised to regulate trade between the United States and the Natives "[f]or the benefit and comfort of the Indians, and for the prevention of injuries or oppressions on the part of the citizens or Indians." The tribes, President Washington, and Secretary of War Henry Knox all were unhappy over white abuses that continued in defiance of the treaties, and became convinced that enforcement legislation was needed.

On August 22, 1789, the President entered the chamber of the Senate and consulted its members on Indian affairs. After reciting the tribes' dissatisfaction, he noted that the Cherokees lived primarily in North Carolina, which had not yet joined the union, and added:

> The commissioners for negotiating with the Southern Indians may be instructed to transmit a message to the Cherokees, stating to them, as far as may be proper, the difficulties arising from the local claims of North Carolina, and to assure them that the United States are not unmindful of the treaty at Hopewell. . . .
>
> The Commissioners may be instructed to transmit messages to the said tribes, containing our assurances of the continuance of the friendship of the United States, and that measures will soon be taken for extending a trade to them agreeably to the treaties of Hopewell.

The President then proceeded to impress upon his listeners the importance of an early agreement with the Creeks. He returned two days later for further consultation. Congress responded the following summer by enacting the Indian Intercourse Act.

Hence, the first three sections of the Act were designed to fulfill the promise of the United States to regulate trade for the benefit of the Indians. Section 4 was, by its terms, designed to effectuate Indian treaties. Section 5—the substantive criminal provision—loosely tracked the language in another provision of the Hopewell pacts, which required that United States citizens who committed crimes in Indian country be tried and punished as if they had committed those crimes against fellow citizens. Provisions in treaties that defined and provided for punishment of crimes were well precedented.

The trade and criminal portions of the Indian Intercourse Act applied to all Native Americans, not merely the Hopewell tribes. But that was because none of the treaties limited their primary benefits to members of the signatory tribes. The trade provisions in the treaties referred generally to "the Indians," and the criminal sections referred to "any Indian." Further, the broad statutory language was appropriate because the government apparently planned to apply the Hopewell language as a template for future agreements: very similar terms were contained in a fourth treaty, signed only a few days later with the Creeks, and in a fifth, concluded the following year with the Cherokees.

A law enacted to execute the Treaty Power cannot be said to represent an interpretation of the Commerce Clause. . . .

# Chapter 3

# Standing, Ripeness, and Mootness

## ASSIGNMENT S-4

### Standing

*STUDY GUIDE:*

- What would have happened if, in addition to refusing to defend DOMA in court, the Department of Justice had also refused to enforce it? Would Windsor have still had standing? Does this raise any concerns?
- Can you identify a fundamental disagreement between Justices Kennedy and Scalia about the source and nature of "the judicial power" that explains their differing stances on standing?

#### UNITED STATES v. WINDSOR

*No. 12-307. | Decided June 26, 2013*

JUSTICE KENNEDY delivered the opinion of the Court.

Two women then resident in New York were married in a lawful ceremony in Ontario, Canada, in 2007. Edith Windsor and Thea Spyer returned to their home in New York City. When Spyer died in 2009, she left her entire estate to Windsor. Windsor sought to claim the estate tax exemption for surviving spouses. She was barred from doing so, however, by a federal law, the Defense of Marriage Act, which excludes a same-sex partner from the definition of "spouse" as that term is used in federal statutes. Windsor paid the taxes but filed suit to challenge the constitutionality of this provision. The United States District Court and the Court of Appeals ruled that this portion of the statute is unconstitutional and ordered the United States to pay Windsor a refund. This Court granted certiorari and now affirms the judgment in Windsor's favor.

I

. . . While the tax refund suit was pending, the Attorney General of the United States notified the Speaker of the House of Representatives, pursuant to 28 U.S.C. §530D, that the Department of Justice would no longer defend the constitutionality of DOMA's §3. Noting that "the Department has previously defended DOMA against . . . challenges involving legally married same-sex couples," the Attorney General informed Congress that "the President has concluded that given a number of factors, including a documented history of discrimination, classifications based on sexual orientation should be subject to a heightened standard of scrutiny." The Department of Justice has submitted many §530D letters over the years refusing to defend laws it deems unconstitutional, when, for instance, a federal court has rejected the Government's defense of a statute and has issued a judgment against it. This case is unusual, however, because the §530D letter was not preceded by an adverse judgment. The letter instead reflected the Executive's own conclusion, relying on a definition still being debated and considered in the courts, that heightened equal protection scrutiny should apply to laws that classify on the basis of sexual orientation.

Although "the President . . . instructed the Department not to defend the statute in *Windsor*," he also decided "that Section 3 will continue to be enforced by the Executive Branch" and that the United States had an "interest in providing Congress a full and fair opportunity to participate in the litigation of those cases." The stated rationale for this dual-track procedure (determination of unconstitutionality coupled with ongoing enforcement) was to "recogniz[e] the judiciary as the final arbiter of the constitutional claims raised."

In response to the notice from the Attorney General, the Bipartisan Legal Advisory Group (BLAG) of the House of Representatives voted to intervene in the litigation to defend the constitutionality of §3 of DOMA. The Department of Justice did not oppose limited intervention by BLAG. . . .

On the merits of the tax refund suit, the District Court ruled against the United States. It held that §3 of DOMA is unconstitutional and ordered the Treasury to refund the tax with interest. Both the Justice Department and BLAG filed notices of appeal, and the Solicitor General filed a petition for certiorari before judgment. Before this Court acted on the petition, the Court of Appeals for the Second Circuit affirmed the District Court's judgment. It applied heightened scrutiny to classifications based on sexual orientation, as both the Department and Windsor had urged. The United States has not complied with the judgment. Windsor has not received her refund, and the Executive Branch continues to enforce §3 of DOMA. In granting certiorari on the question of the constitutionality of §3 of DOMA, the Court requested argument on two additional questions: whether the United States' agreement with Windsor's legal position precludes further review and whether BLAG has standing to appeal the case. All parties agree that the Court has jurisdiction to decide this case; and, with the case in that framework, the Court appointed Professor Vicki Jackson as *amicus curiae* to argue the position that the Court lacks jurisdiction to hear the dispute. She has ably discharged her duties. . . .

## II

It is appropriate to begin by addressing whether either the Government or BLAG, or both of them, were entitled to appeal to the Court of Appeals and later to seek certiorari and appear as parties here. There is no dispute that when this case was in the District Court it presented a concrete disagreement between opposing parties, a dispute suitable for judicial resolution. "[A] taxpayer has standing to challenge the collection of a specific tax assessment as unconstitutional; being forced to pay such a tax causes a real and immediate economic injury to the individual taxpayer." *Hein v. Freedom From Religion Foundation, Inc.* (2007) (plurality opinion) (emphasis deleted). Windsor suffered a redressable injury when she was required to pay estate taxes from which, in her view, she was exempt but for the alleged invalidity of §3 of DOMA.

The decision of the Executive not to defend the constitutionality of §3 in court while continuing to deny refunds and to assess deficiencies does introduce a complication. Even though the Executive's current position was announced before the District Court entered its judgment, the Government's agreement with Windsor's position would not have deprived the District Court of jurisdiction to entertain and resolve the refund suit; for her injury (failure to obtain a refund allegedly required by law) was concrete, persisting, and unredressed. The Government's position—agreeing with Windsor's legal contention but refusing to give it effect—meant that there was a justiciable controversy between the parties, despite what the claimant would find to be an inconsistency in that stance. Windsor, the Government, BLAG, and the *amicus* appear to agree upon that point. The disagreement is over the standing of the parties, or aspiring parties, to take an appeal in the Court of Appeals and to appear as parties in further proceedings in this Court.

The *amicus*' position is that, given the Government's concession that §3 is unconstitutional, once the District Court ordered the refund the case should have ended; and the *amicus* argues the Court of Appeals should have dismissed the appeal. The *amicus* submits that once the President agreed with Windsor's legal position and the District Court issued its judgment, the parties were no longer adverse. From this standpoint the United States was a prevailing party below, just as Windsor was. Accordingly, the *amicus* reasons, it is inappropriate for this Court to grant certiorari and proceed to rule on the merits; for the United States seeks no redress from the judgment entered against it.

This position, however, elides the distinction between two principles: the jurisdictional requirements of Article III and the prudential limits on its exercise. See *Warth v. Seldin* (1975). The latter are "essentially matters of judicial self-governance." The Court has kept these two strands separate: "Article III standing, which enforces the Constitution's case-or-controversy requirement, see *Lujan v. Defenders of Wildlife* (1992); and prudential standing, which embodies "'judicially self-imposed limits on the exercise of federal jurisdiction,' *Allen* [*v. Wright,*] (1984)." *Elk Grove Unified School Dist. v. Newdow* (2004).

The requirements of Article III standing are familiar:

> First, the plaintiff must have suffered an "injury in fact"—an invasion of a legally protected interest which is (a) concrete and particularized, and (b) "actual or imminent, not "conjectural or hypothetical." Second, there must be a causal connection between the injury and the conduct complained of—the injury has to be "fairly . . . trace[able] to the challenged action of the defendant, and not . . . th[e] result [of]

> the independent action of some third party not before the court." Third, it must be "likely," as opposed to merely "speculative," that the injury will be "redressed by a favorable decision." *Lujan*.

Rules of prudential standing, by contrast, are more flexible "rule[s] . . . of federal appellate practice," *Deposit Guaranty Nat. Bank v. Roper* (1980), designed to protect the courts from "decid[ing] abstract questions of wide public significance even [when] other governmental institutions may be more competent to address the questions and even though judicial intervention may be unnecessary to protect individual rights." *Warth*.

In this case the United States retains a stake sufficient to support Article III jurisdiction on appeal and in proceedings before this Court. The judgment in question orders the United States to pay Windsor the refund she seeks. An order directing the Treasury to pay money is "a real and immediate economic injury," *Hein*, indeed as real and immediate as an order directing an individual to pay a tax. That the Executive may welcome this order to pay the refund if it is accompanied by the constitutional ruling it wants does not eliminate the injury to the national Treasury if payment is made, or to the taxpayer if it is not. The judgment orders the United States to pay money that it would not disburse but for the court's order. The Government of the United States has a valid legal argument that it is injured even if the Executive disagrees with §3 of DOMA, which results in Windsor's liability for the tax. Windsor's ongoing claim for funds that the United States refuses to pay thus establishes a controversy sufficient for Article III jurisdiction. It would be a different case if the Executive had taken the further step of paying Windsor the refund to which she was entitled under the District Court's ruling.

This Court confronted a comparable case in *INS v. Chadha* (1983). A statute by its terms allowed one House of Congress to order the Immigration and Naturalization Service (INS) to deport the respondent Chadha. There, as here, the Executive determined that the statute was unconstitutional, and "the INS presented the Executive's views on the constitutionality of the House action to the Court of Appeals." The INS, however, continued to abide by the statute, and "the INS brief to the Court of Appeals did not alter the agency's decision to comply with the House action ordering deportation of Chadha." This Court held "that the INS was sufficiently aggrieved by the Court of Appeals decision prohibiting it from taking action it would otherwise take," regardless of whether the agency welcomed the judgment. The necessity of a "case or controversy" to satisfy Article III was defined as a requirement that the Court's "decision will have real meaning: if we rule for Chadha, he will not be deported; if we uphold [the statute], the INS will execute its order and deport him." This conclusion was not dictum. It was a necessary predicate to the Court's holding that "prior to Congress' intervention, there was adequate Art. III adverseness." The holdings of cases are instructive, and the words of *Chadha* make clear its holding that the refusal of the Executive to provide the relief sought suffices to preserve a justiciable dispute as required by Article III. In short, even where "the Government largely agree[s] with the opposing party on the merits of the controversy," there is sufficient adverseness and an "adequate basis for jurisdiction in the fact that the Government intended to enforce the challenged law against that party."

It is true that "[a] party who receives all that he has sought generally is not aggrieved by the judgment affording the relief and cannot appeal from it." *Roper*. But this rule "does not have its source in the jurisdictional limitations of Art. III. In an appropriate case, appeal may be permitted . . . at the behest of the party who has prevailed on the merits, so long as that party retains a stake in the appeal satisfying the requirements of Art. III." *Roper*.

While these principles suffice to show that this case presents a justiciable controversy under Article III, the prudential problems inherent in the Executive's unusual position require some further discussion. The Executive's agreement with Windsor's legal argument raises the risk that instead of a "real, earnest and vital controversy," the Court faces a "friendly, non-adversary, proceeding . . . [in which] a party beaten in the legislature [seeks to] transfer to the courts an inquiry as to the constitutionality of the legislative act." *Ashwander v. TVA* (1936) (Brandeis, J., concurring). Even when Article III permits the exercise of federal jurisdiction, prudential considerations demand that the Court insist upon "that concrete adverseness which sharpens the presentation of issues upon which the court so largely depends for illumination of difficult constitutional questions." *Baker v. Carr* (1962).

There are, of course, reasons to hear a case and issue a ruling even when one party is reluctant to prevail in its position. Unlike Article III requirements — which must be satisfied by the parties before judicial consideration is appropriate — the relevant prudential factors that counsel against hearing this case are subject to "countervailing considerations [that] may outweigh the concerns underlying the usual reluctance to exert judicial power." *Warth*. One consideration is the extent to which adversarial presentation of the issues is assured by the participation of *amici curiae* prepared to defend with vigor the constitutionality of the legislative act. With respect to this prudential aspect of standing as well, the *Chadha* Court encountered a similar situation. It noted that "there may be prudential, as opposed to Art. III, concerns about sanctioning the adjudication of [this case] in the absence of any participant supporting the validity of [the statute]. The Court of Appeals properly dispelled any such concerns by inviting and accepting briefs from both Houses of Congress." *Chadha* was not an anomaly in this respect. The Court adopts the practice of entertaining arguments made by an *amicus* when the Solicitor General confesses error with respect to a judgment below, even if the confession is in effect an admission that an Act of Congress is unconstitutional.

In the case now before the Court the attorneys for BLAG present a substantial argument for the constitutionality of §3 of DOMA. BLAG's sharp adversarial presentation of the issues satisfies the prudential concerns that otherwise might counsel against hearing an appeal from a decision with which the principal parties agree. Were this Court to hold that prudential rules require it to dismiss the case, and, in consequence, that the Court of Appeals erred in failing to dismiss it as well, extensive litigation would ensue. The district courts in 94 districts throughout the Nation would be without precedential guidance not only in tax refund suits but also in cases involving the whole of DOMA's sweep involving over 1,000 federal statutes and a myriad of federal regulations. For instance, the opinion of the Court of Appeals for the First Circuit, addressing the validity of DOMA in a case involving regulations of the Department of Health and Human Services, likely would be vacated with instructions to dismiss, its ruling and guidance also then erased. Rights and privileges of hundreds of thousands of persons would be adversely affected, pending a case in which all prudential concerns about justiciability are absent. That numerical prediction may not be certain, but it is certain that the cost in judicial resources and expense of litigation for all persons adversely affected would be immense. True, the very extent of DOMA's mandate means that at some point a case likely would arise without the prudential concerns raised here; but the costs, uncertainties, and alleged harm and injuries likely would continue for a time measured in years before the issue is resolved. In these unusual and urgent circumstances, the very term "prudential" counsels that it is a proper exercise of the Court's responsibility to take jurisdiction. For these reasons, the prudential and Article III requirements are met here. . . .

The Court's conclusion that this petition may be heard on the merits does not imply that no difficulties would ensue if this were a common practice in ordinary cases. The Executive's failure to defend the constitutionality of an Act of Congress based on a constitutional theory not yet established in judicial decisions has created a procedural dilemma. On the one hand, as noted, the Government's agreement with Windsor raises questions about the propriety of entertaining a suit in which it seeks affirmance of an order invalidating a federal law and ordering the United States to pay money. On the other hand, if the Executive's agreement with a plaintiff that a law is unconstitutional is enough to preclude judicial review, then the Supreme Court's primary role in determining the constitutionality of a law that has inflicted real injury on a plaintiff who has brought a justiciable legal claim would become only secondary to the President's. This would undermine the clear dictate of the separation-of-powers principle that when an Act of Congress is alleged to conflict with the Constitution, "[i]t is emphatically the province and duty of the judicial department to say what the law is." *Marbury v. Madison* (1803). Similarly, with respect to the legislative power, when Congress has passed a statute and a President has signed it, it poses grave challenges to the separation of powers for the Executive at a particular moment to be able to nullify Congress' enactment solely on its own initiative and without any determination from the Court.

The Court's jurisdictional holding, it must be underscored, does not mean the arguments for dismissing this dispute on prudential grounds lack substance. Yet the difficulty the Executive faces should be acknowledged. When the Executive makes a principled determination that a statute is unconstitutional, it faces a difficult choice. Still, there is no suggestion here that it is appropriate for the Executive as a matter of course to challenge statutes in the judicial forum rather than making the case to Congress for their amendment or repeal. The integrity of the political process would be at risk if difficult constitutional issues were simply referred to the Court as a routine exercise. But this case is not routine. And the capable defense of the law by BLAG ensures that these prudential issues do not cloud the merits question, which is one of immediate importance to the Federal Government and to hundreds of thousands of persons. These circumstances support the Court's decision to proceed to the merits.

JUSTICE SCALIA, with whom JUSTICE THOMAS joins, and with whom THE CHIEF JUSTICE joins as to Part I, dissenting. . . .

This case is about power in several respects. It is about the power of our people to govern themselves, and the power of this Court to pronounce the law. Today's opinion aggrandizes the latter, with the predictable consequence of diminishing the former. We have no power to decide this case. And even if we did, we have no power under the Constitution to invalidate this democratically adopted legislation. The Court's errors on both points spring forth from the same diseased root: an exalted conception of the role of this institution in America.

I

A

The Court is eager—*hungry*—to tell everyone its view of the legal question at the heart of this case. Standing in the way is an obstacle, a technicality of little interest to anyone but the people of We the People, who created it as a barrier against judges' intrusion into their lives. They gave judges, in Article III, only the "judicial Power," a power to decide not abstract questions but real, concrete "Cases" and "Controversies." Yet the plaintiff and the Government agree entirely on what should happen in this lawsuit. They agree that the court below got it right; and they agreed in the court below that the court below that one got it right as well. What, then, are we *doing* here? The answer lies at the heart of the jurisdictional portion of today's opinion, where a single sentence lays bare the majority's vision of our role. The Court says that we have the power to decide this case because if we did not, then our "primary role in determining the constitutionality of a law" (at least one that "has inflicted real injury on a plaintiff") would "become only secondary to the President's." But wait, the reader wonders—Windsor won below, and so *cured* her injury, and the President was glad to see it. True, says the majority, but judicial review must march on regardless, lest we "undermine the clear dictate of the separation-of-powers principle that when an Act of Congress is alleged to conflict with the Constitution, it is emphatically the province and duty of the judicial department to say what the law is."

That is jaw-dropping. It is an assertion of judicial supremacy over the people's Representatives in Congress and the Executive. It envisions a Supreme Court standing (or rather enthroned) at the apex of government, empowered to decide all constitutional questions, always and everywhere "primary" in its role.

This image of the Court would have been unrecognizable to those who wrote and ratified our national charter. They knew well the dangers of "primary" power, and so created branches of government that would be "perfectly co-ordinate by the terms of their common commission," none of which branches could "pretend to an exclusive or superior right of settling the boundaries between their respective powers." The Federalist, No. 49 (J. Madison). The people did this to protect themselves. They did it to guard their right to self-rule against the black-robed supremacy that today's majority finds so attractive. So it was that Madison could confidently state, with no fear of contradiction, that there was nothing of "greater intrinsic value" or "stamped with the authority of more enlightened patrons of liberty" than a government of separate and coordinate powers. *Id.*, No. 47.

For this reason we are quite forbidden to say what the law is whenever (as today's opinion asserts) "an Act of Congress is alleged to conflict with the Constitution." We can do so only when that allegation will determine the outcome of a lawsuit, and is contradicted by the other party. The "judicial Power" is not, as the majority believes, the power "to say what the law is," giving the Supreme Court the "primary role in determining the constitutionality of laws." The majority must have in mind one of the foreign constitutions that pronounces such primacy for its constitutional court and allows that primacy to be exercised in contexts other than a lawsuit. See, *e.g.,* Basic Law for the Federal Republic of Germany, Art. 93. The judicial power as Americans have understood it (and their English ancestors before them) is the power to adjudicate, with conclusive effect, disputed government claims (civil or criminal) against private persons, and disputed claims by private persons against the government or other private persons. Sometimes (though not always) the parties before the court disagree not with regard to the facts of their case (or not *only* with regard to the facts) but with regard to the applicable law—in which event (and *only* in which event) it becomes the "province and duty of the judicial department to say what the law is."

In other words, declaring the compatibility of state or federal laws with the Constitution is not only not the "primary role" of this Court, it is not a separate, free-standing role *at all.* We perform that role incidentally—by accident, as it were—when that is necessary to resolve the dispute before us. Then, and only then, does it become "the province and duty of the judicial department to say what the law is." That is why, in 1793, we politely declined the Washington Administration's request to "say what the law is" on a particular treaty matter that was not the subject of a concrete legal controversy. And that is why, as our opinions have said, some questions of law will *never* be presented to this Court, because there will never be anyone with standing to bring a lawsuit. See *Schlesinger v. Reservists Comm. to Stop the War* (1974); *United States v. Richardson* (1974). As Justice Brandeis put it, we cannot "pass upon the constitutionality of legislation in a friendly, non-adversary, proceeding"; absent a "real, earnest and vital controversy between individuals," we have neither any work to do nor any power to do it. *Ashwander v. TVA* (1936) (concurring opinion). Our authority begins and ends with the need to adjudge the rights of an injured party who stands before us seeking redress. *Lujan v. Defenders of Wildlife* (1992).That is completely absent here. Windsor's injury was cured by the judgment in her favor. And while, in ordinary circumstances, the United States is injured by a directive to pay a tax refund, this suit is far from ordinary. Whatever injury the United States has suffered will surely not be redressed by the action that it, as a litigant, asks us to take. The final sentence of the Solicitor General's brief on the merits reads: "For the foregoing reasons, the judgment of the court of appeals *should be affirmed*." That will not cure the Government's injury, but carve it into stone. One could spend many fruitless afternoons ransacking our library for any other petitioner's brief seeking an affirmance of the judgment against it. What the petitioner United States asks us to do in the case before us is exactly what the respondent Windsor asks us to do: not to provide relief from the judgment below but to say that that judgment was correct. And the same was true in the Court of Appeals: Neither party sought to undo the judgment for Windsor, and so that court should have dismissed the appeal (just as we should dismiss) for lack of jurisdiction. Since both parties agreed with the judgment of the District Court for the Southern District of New York, the suit should have ended there. The further proceedings have been a contrivance, having no object in mind except to elevate a District Court judgment that has no precedential effect in other courts, to one that has precedential effect throughout the Second Circuit, and then (in this Court) precedential effect throughout the United States.

We have never before agreed to speak—to "say what the law is"—where there is no controversy before us. In the more than two centuries that this Court has existed as an institution, we have never suggested that we have the power to decide a question when every party agrees with both its nominal opponent *and the court below* on that question's answer. The United States reluctantly conceded that at oral argument. See Tr. of Oral Arg. 19-20.

The closest we have ever come to what the Court blesses today was our opinion in *INS v. Chadha* (1983). But in that case, two parties to the litigation disagreed with the position of the United States and with the court below: the House and Senate, which had intervened in the case. Because *Chadha* concerned the validity of a mode of congressional action—the one-house legislative veto—the House and Senate were threatened with destruction of what they claimed to be one of their institutional powers. The Executive choosing not to defend that power,[1] we permitted the House and Senate to intervene. Nothing like that is present here.

To be sure, the Court in *Chadha* said that statutory aggrieved-party status was "not altered by the fact that the Executive may agree with the holding that

---

1. There the Justice Department's refusal to defend the legislation was in accord with its longstanding (and entirely reasonable) practice of declining to defend legislation that in its view infringes upon Presidential powers. There is no justification for the Justice Department's abandoning the law in the present case. The majority opinion makes a point of scolding the President for his "failure to defend the constitutionality of an Act of Congress based on a constitutional theory not yet established in judicial decisions." But the rebuke is tongue-in-cheek, for the majority gladly gives the President what he wants. Contrary to all precedent, it decides this case (and even decides it the way the President wishes) *despite* his abandonment of the defense and the consequent absence of a case or controversy.

the statute in question is unconstitutional." But in a footnote to that statement, the Court acknowledged Article III's separate requirement of a "justiciable case or controversy," and stated that *this* requirement was satisfied "because of the presence of the two Houses of Congress as adverse parties." . . . When a private party has a judicial decree safely in hand to prevent his injury, additional judicial action requires that a party injured by the decree *seek to undo it*. In *Chadha,* the intervening House and Senate fulfilled that requirement. Here no one does.

The majority's discussion of the requirements of Article III bears no resemblance to our jurisprudence. It accuses the *amicus* (appointed to argue against our jurisdiction) of "elid[ing] the distinction between . . . the jurisdictional requirements of Article III and the prudential limits on its exercise." It then proceeds to call the requirement of adverseness a "prudential" aspect of standing. *Of standing.* That is incomprehensible. A plaintiff (or appellant) can have all the standing in the world—satisfying all three standing requirements of *Lujan* that the majority so carefully quotes—and yet no Article III controversy may be before the court. Article III requires not just a plaintiff (or appellant) who has standing to complain but *an opposing party* who denies the validity of the complaint. It is not the *amicus* that has done the eliding of distinctions, but the majority, calling the quite separate Article III requirement of adverseness between the parties an element (which it then pronounces a "prudential" element) of standing. The question here is not whether, as the majority puts it, "the United States retains a stake sufficient to support Article III jurisdiction," the question is whether there is any controversy (which requires *contradiction*) between the United States and Ms. Windsor. There is not.

I find it wryly amusing that the majority seeks to dismiss the requirement of party-adverseness as nothing more than a "prudential" aspect of the sole Article III requirement of standing. (Relegating a jurisdictional requirement to "prudential" status is a wondrous device, enabling courts to ignore the requirement whenever they believe it "prudent"—which is to say, a good idea.) Half a century ago, a Court similarly bent upon announcing its view regarding the constitutionality of a federal statute achieved that goal by effecting a remarkably similar *but completely opposite* distortion of the principles limiting our jurisdiction. The Court's notorious opinion in *Flast v. Cohen* (1968), held that *standing* was merely an element (which it pronounced to be a "prudential" element) of the sole Article III requirement of *adverseness*. We have been living with the chaos created by that power-grabbing decision ever since, see *Hein v. Freedom From Religion Foundation, Inc.* (2007), as we will have to live with the chaos created by this one. . . .

It may be argued that if what we say is true some Presidential determinations that statutes are unconstitutional will not be subject to our review. That is as it should be, when both the President and the plaintiff agree that the statute is unconstitutional. Where the Executive is enforcing an unconstitutional law, suit will of course lie; but if, in that suit, the Executive admits the unconstitutionality of the law, the litigation should end in an order or a consent decree enjoining enforcement. This suit saw the light of day only because the President enforced the Act (and thus gave Windsor standing to sue) even though he believed it unconstitutional. He could have equally chosen (more appropriately, some would say) neither to enforce nor to defend the statute he believed to be unconstitutional, see Presidential Authority to Decline to Execute Unconstitutional Statutes, 18 Op. Off. Legal Counsel 199 (Nov. 2, 1994)—in which event Windsor would not have been injured, the District Court could not have refereed this friendly scrimmage, and the Executive's determination of unconstitutionality would have escaped this Court's desire to blurt out its view of the law. The matter would have been left, as so many matters ought to be left, to a tug of war between the President and the Congress, which has innumerable means (up to and including impeachment) of compelling the President to enforce the laws it has written. Or the President could have evaded presentation of the constitutional issue to this Court simply by declining to appeal the District Court and Court of Appeals dispositions he agreed with. Be sure of this much: If a President wants to insulate his judgment of unconstitutionality from our review, he can. What the views urged in this dissent produce is not insulation from judicial review but insulation from Executive contrivance.

The majority brandishes the famous sentence from *Marbury v. Madison* (1803) that "[i]t is emphatically the province and duty of the judicial department to say what the law is." But that sentence neither says nor implies that it is *always* the province and duty of the Court to say what the law is—much less that its responsibility in that regard is a "primary" one. The very next sentence of Chief Justice Marshall's opinion makes the crucial qualification that today's majority ignores: "*Those who apply the rule to particular cases,* must of necessity expound and interpret that rule." (emphasis added). Only when a "particular case" is before us—that is, a controversy that it is our business to resolve under Article III—do we have the province and duty to pronounce the law. For the views of our early Court more precisely addressing the question before us here, the majority ought instead to have consulted the opinion of Chief Justice Taney in *Lord v. Veazie* (1850):

> The objection in the case before us is . . . that the plaintiff and defendant have the same interest, and that interest adverse and in conflict with the interest of third persons, whose rights would be seriously affected if the question of law was decided in the manner that both of the parties to this suit desire it to be. A judgment entered under such circumstances, and for such purposes, is a mere form. The whole proceeding was in contempt of the court, and highly reprehensible. . . . A judgment in form, thus procured, in the eye of the law is no judgment of the court. It is a nullity, and no writ of error will lie upon it. This writ is, therefore, dismissed.

There is, in the words of *Marbury,* no "necessity [to] expound and interpret" the law in this case; just a desire to place this Court at the center of the Nation's life. . . .

B

A few words in response to the theory of jurisdiction set forth in Justice Alito's dissent: Though less far reaching in its consequences than the majority's conversion of constitutionally required adverseness into a discretionary element of standing, the theory of that dissent similarly elevates the Court to the "primary" determiner of constitutional questions involving the separation of powers, and, to boot, increases the power of the most dangerous branch: the "legislative department," which by its nature "draw [s] all power into its impetuous vortex." The Federalist, No. 48, at 309 (J. Madison). Heretofore in our national history, the President's failure to "take Care that the Laws be faithfully executed," U.S. Const., Art. II, §3, could only be brought before a judicial tribunal by someone whose concrete interests were harmed by that alleged failure. Justice Alito would create a system in which Congress can hale the Executive before the courts not only to vindicate its own institutional powers to act, but to correct a perceived inadequacy in the execution of its laws.[2] This would lay to rest Tocqueville's praise of our judicial system as one which "intimately bind[s] the case made for the law with the case made for one man," one in which legislation is "no longer exposed to the daily aggression of the parties," and in which "[t]he political question that [the judge] must resolve is linked to the interest" of private litigants. A. de Tocqueville, Democracy in America 97 (H. Mansfield & D. Winthrop eds. 2000). That would be replaced by a system in which Congress and the Executive can pop immediately into court, in their institutional capacity, whenever the President refuses to implement a statute he believes to be unconstitutional, and whenever he implements a law in a manner that is not to Congress's liking.

Justice Alito's notion of standing will likewise enormously shrink the area to which "judicial censure, exercised by the courts on legislation, cannot extend." *ibid.* For example, a bare majority of both Houses could bring into court the assertion that the Executive's implementation of welfare programs is too generous—a failure that no other litigant would have standing to complain about. . . .

To be sure, if Congress cannot invoke our authority in the way that Justice Alito proposes, then its only recourse is to confront the President directly. Unimaginable evil this is not. Our system is *designed* for confrontation. That is

---

2. Justice Alito attempts to limit his argument by claiming that Congress is injured (and can therefore appeal) when its statute is held unconstitutional without Presidential defense, but is *not* injured when its statute is held unconstitutional *despite* Presidential defense. I do not understand that line. The injury to Congress is the same whether the President has defended the statute or not. And if the injury is threatened, why should Congress not be able to participate in the suit from the beginning, just as the President can? And if having a statute declared unconstitutional (and therefore inoperative) by a court is an injury, why is it not an injury when a statute is declared unconstitutional by the President and rendered inoperative by his consequent failure to enforce it? Or when the President simply declines to enforce it without opining on its constitutionality? If it is the *inoperativeness* that constitutes the injury—the "impairment of [the legislative] function," as Justice Alito puts it—it should make no difference which of the other two branches inflicts it, and whether the Constitution is the pretext. A principled and predictable system of jurisprudence cannot rest upon a shifting concept of injury, designed to support standing when we would like it. . . .

what "[a]mbition . . . counteract[ing] ambition," The Federalist, No. 51, at 322 (J. Madison), is all about. If majorities in both Houses of Congress care enough about the matter, they have available innumerable ways to compel executive action without a lawsuit—from refusing to confirm Presidential appointees to the elimination of funding. (Nothing says "enforce the Act" quite like ". . . or you will have money for little else.") But the condition is crucial; Congress must care enough to act against the President itself, not merely enough to instruct its lawyers to ask *us* to do so. Placing the Constitution's entirely anticipated political arm wrestling into permanent judicial receivership does not do the system a favor. And by the way, if the President loses the lawsuit but does not faithfully implement the Court's decree, just as he did not faithfully implement Congress's statute, what then? Only Congress can bring him to heel by . . . what do you think? Yes: a direct confrontation with the President.

JUSTICE ALITO . . . dissenting. . . .

In my view, the United States clearly is not a proper petitioner in this case. The United States does not ask us to overturn the judgment of the court below or to alter that judgment in any way. Quite to the contrary, the United States argues emphatically in favor of the correctness of that judgment. We have never before reviewed a decision at the sole behest of a party that took such a position, and to do so would be to render an advisory opinion, in violation of Article III's dictates. For the reasons given in Justice Scalia's dissent, I do not find the Court's arguments to the contrary to be persuasive. Whether the Bipartisan Legal Advisory Group of the House of Representatives (BLAG) has standing to petition is a much more difficult question. It is also a significantly closer question than whether the intervenors in *Hollingsworth v. Perry,* which the Court also decides today—have standing to appeal. It is remarkable that the Court has simultaneously decided that the United States, which "receive[d] all that [it] ha[d] sought" below, *Deposit Guaranty Nat. Bank v. Roper* (1980), is a proper petitioner in this case but that the intervenors in *Hollingsworth,* who represent the party that lost in the lower court, are not. In my view, both the *Hollingsworth* intervenors and BLAG have standing. . . .

A party invoking the Court's authority has a sufficient stake to permit it to appeal when it has "'suffered an injury in fact' that is caused by 'the conduct complained of' and that 'will be redressed by a favorable decision.'" *Camreta v. Greene* (2011) (quoting *Lujan v. Defenders of Wildlife* (1992)). In the present case, the House of Representatives, which has authorized BLAG to represent its interests in this matter, suffered just such an injury. In *INS v. Chadha* (1983), the Court held that the two Houses of Congress were "proper parties" to file a petition in defense of the constitutionality of the one-house veto statute. Accordingly, the Court granted and decided petitions by both the Senate and the House, in addition to the Executive's petition. That the two Houses had standing to petition is not surprising: The Court of Appeals' decision in *Chadha,* by holding the one-house veto to be unconstitutional, had limited Congress' power to legislate. In discussing Article III standing, the Court suggested that Congress suffered a similar injury whenever federal legislation it had passed was struck down, noting that it had "long held that Congress is the proper party to defend the validity of a statute when an agency of government, as a defendant charged with enforcing the statute, agrees with plaintiffs that the statute is inapplicable or unconstitutional."

The United States attempts to distinguish *Chadha* on the ground that it "involved an unusual statute that vested the House and the Senate themselves each with special procedural rights—namely, the right effectively to veto Executive action." But that is a distinction without a difference: just as the Court of Appeals decision that the *Chadha* Court affirmed impaired Congress' power by striking down the one-house veto, so the Second Circuit's decision here impairs Congress' legislative power by striking down an Act of Congress. The United States has not explained why the fact that the impairment at issue in *Chadha* was "special" or "procedural" has any relevance to whether Congress suffered an injury. Indeed, because legislating is Congress' central function, any impairment of that function is a more grievous injury than the impairment of a procedural add-on. . . .

Both the United States and the Court-appointed *amicus* err in arguing that *Raines v. Byrd* (1997), is to the contrary. . . . *Raines* dealt with individual Members of Congress and specifically pointed to the individual Members' lack of institutional endorsement as a sign of their standing problem: "We attach some importance to the fact that appellees have not been authorized to represent their respective Houses of Congress in this action, and indeed both Houses actively oppose their suit." . . . Here, by contrast, passage by the House was needed for DOMA to become law. U.S. Const., Art. I, §7 (bicameralism and presentment requirements for legislation).

I appreciate the argument that the Constitution confers on the President alone the authority to defend federal law in litigation, but in my view, as I have explained, that argument is contrary to the Court's holding in *Chadha,* and it is certainly contrary to the *Chadha* Court's endorsement of the principle that "Congress is the proper party to defend the validity of a statute" when the Executive refuses to do so on constitutional grounds. Accordingly, in the narrow category of cases in which a court strikes down an Act of Congress and the Executive declines to defend the Act, Congress both has standing to defend the undefended statute and is a proper party to do so. . . .

***Study Guide:***

- In the next case, Justices Kennedy and Alito argued in favor of standing as they had in *Windsor*. Chief Justice Roberts and Justice Scalia argued against standing in both cases. By contrast, Justices Breyer, Sotomayor, and Kagan switched from standing in *Windsor* to no standing here, while Justice Thomas switched from no standing in *Windsor* to standing here. Can these shifts in the line-ups be explained by differing philosophies on the doctrine of standing, as opposed to a desire to reach different outcomes in each case?

- If an initiative's proponents lack standing to defend it from constitutional challenge when the government refuses to do so, does this undermine the popular check on government that is supposed to be provided by popular initiatives? Should doctrine of federal standing reflect this difficulty?
- Is there any way for states with initiatives to fix this problem consistent with Chief Justice Roberts' opinion?
- Can you see the continuing relevance of the differing concepts of sovereignty we have seen discussed in previous chapters?

## HOLLINGSWORTH v. PERRY

*No. 12-144.* | *Decided June 26, 2013*

CHIEF JUSTICE ROBERTS delivered the opinion of the Court.

The public is currently engaged in an active political debate over whether same-sex couples should be allowed to marry. That question has also given rise to litigation. In this case, petitioners, who oppose same-sex marriage, ask us to decide whether the Equal Protection Clause "prohibits the State of California from defining marriage as the union of a man and a woman." Pet. for Cert. i. Respondents, same-sex couples who wish to marry, view the issue in somewhat different terms: For them, it is whether California—having previously recognized the right of same-sex couples to marry—may reverse that decision through a referendum. Federal courts have authority under the Constitution to answer such questions only if necessary to do so in the course of deciding an actual "case" or "controversy." As used in the Constitution, those words do not include every sort of dispute, but only those "historically viewed as capable of resolution through the judicial process." *Flast v. Cohen* (1968). This is an essential limit on our power: It ensures that we act *as judges,* and do not engage in policymaking properly left to elected representatives.

For there to be such a case or controversy, it is not enough that the party invoking the power of the court have a keen interest in the issue. That party must also have "standing," which requires, among other things, that it have suffered a concrete and particularized injury. Because we find that petitioners do not have standing, we have no authority to decide this case on the merits, and neither did the Ninth Circuit.

### I

In 2008, the California Supreme Court held that limiting the official designation of marriage to opposite-sex couples violated the equal protection clause of the California Constitution. *In re Marriage Cases* (Cal. 2008) Later that year, California voters passed the ballot initiative at the center of this dispute, known as Proposition 8. That proposition amended the California Constitution to provide that "[o]nly marriage between a man and a woman is valid or recognized in California." Cal. Const., Art. I, §7.5. Shortly thereafter, the California

Supreme Court rejected a procedural challenge to the amendment, and held that the Proposition was properly enacted under California law. *Strauss v. Horton* (Cal. 2009). According to the California Supreme Court, Proposition 8 created a "narrow and limited exception" to the state constitutional rights otherwise guaranteed to same-sex couples. Under California law, same-sex couples have a right to enter into relationships recognized by the State as "domestic partnerships," which carry "the same rights, protections, and benefits, and shall be subject to the same responsibilities, obligations, and duties under law . . . as are granted to and imposed upon spouses." Cal. Fam. Code Ann. §297.5(a) (2004). In *In re Marriage Cases,* the California Supreme Court concluded that the California Constitution further guarantees same-sex couples "all of the constitutionally based incidents of marriage," including the right to have that marriage "officially recognized" as such by the State. Proposition 8, the court explained in *Strauss,* left those rights largely undisturbed, reserving only "the official *designation* of the term 'marriage' for the union of opposite-sex couples as a matter of state constitutional law."

Respondents, two same-sex couples who wish to marry, filed suit in federal court, challenging Proposition 8 under the Due Process and Equal Protection Clauses of the Fourteenth Amendment to the Federal Constitution. The complaint named as defendants California's Governor, attorney general, and various other state and local officials responsible for enforcing California's marriage laws. Those officials refused to defend the law, although they have continued to enforce it throughout this litigation. The District Court allowed petitioners — the official proponents of the initiative — to intervene to defend it. After a 12-day bench trial, the District Court declared Proposition 8 unconstitutional, permanently enjoining the California officials named as defendants from enforcing the law, and "directing the official defendants that all persons under their control or supervision" shall not enforce it. *Perry v. Schwarzenegger* (N.D. Cal. 2010). Those officials elected not to appeal the District Court order. When petitioners did, the Ninth Circuit asked them to address "why this appeal should not be dismissed for lack of Article III standing." *Perry v. Schwarzenegger* (CA9, Aug. 16, 2010). After briefing and argument, the Ninth Circuit certified a question to the California Supreme Court:

> Whether under Article II, Section 8 of the California Constitution, or otherwise under California law, the official proponents of an initiative measure possess either a particularized interest in the initiative's validity or the authority to assert the State's interest in the initiative's validity, which would enable them to defend the constitutionality of the initiative upon its adoption or appeal a judgment invalidating the initiative, when the public officials charged with that duty refuse to do so.

The California Supreme Court agreed to decide the certified question, and answered in the affirmative. Without addressing whether the proponents have a particularized interest of their own in an initiative's validity, the court concluded that "[i]n a postelection challenge to a voter-approved initiative measure, the official proponents of the initiative are authorized under California law to appear and assert the state's interest in the initiative's validity and to appeal a judgment invalidating the measure when the public officials who ordinarily defend the measure or appeal such a judgment decline to do so." *Perry v. Brown* (CA9, 2011).

Relying on that answer, the Ninth Circuit concluded that petitioners had standing under federal law to defend the constitutionality of Proposition 8. California, it reasoned, " 'has standing to defend the constitutionality of its [laws],' " and States have the "prerogative, as independent sovereigns, to decide for themselves who may assert their interests." *Perry v. Brown* (CA9, 2012). "All a federal court need determine is that the state has suffered a harm sufficient to confer standing and that the party seeking to invoke the jurisdiction of the court is authorized by the state to represent its interest in remedying that harm."

On the merits, the Ninth Circuit affirmed the District Court. The court held the Proposition unconstitutional under the rationale of our decision in *Romer v. Evans* (1996). In the Ninth Circuit's view, *Romer* stands for the proposition that "the Equal Protection Clause requires the state to have a legitimate reason for withdrawing a right or benefit *from one group but not others,* whether or not it was required to confer that right or benefit in the first place." The Ninth Circuit concluded that "taking away the official designation" of "marriage" from same-sex couples, while continuing to afford those couples all the rights and obligations of marriage, did not further any legitimate interest of the State. Proposition 8, in the court's view, violated the Equal Protection Clause because it served no purpose "but to impose on gays and lesbians, through the public law, a majority's private disapproval of them and their relationships."

We granted certiorari to review that determination, and directed that the parties also brief and argue "Whether petitioners have standing under Article III, §2, of the Constitution in this case."

## II

Article III of the Constitution confines the judicial power of federal courts to deciding actual "Cases" or "Controversies." §2. One essential aspect of this requirement is that any person invoking the power of a federal court must demonstrate standing to do so. This requires the litigant to prove that he has suffered a concrete and particularized injury that is fairly traceable to the challenged conduct, and is likely to be redressed by a favorable judicial decision. *Lujan v. Defenders of Wildlife* (1992). In other words, for a federal court to have authority under the Constitution to settle a dispute, the party before it must seek a remedy for a personal and tangible harm. "The presence of a disagreement, however sharp and acrimonious it may be, is insufficient by itself to meet Art. III's requirements." [*Diamond v. Charles* (1986).] The doctrine of standing, we recently explained, "serves to prevent the judicial process from being used to usurp the powers of the political branches." *Clapper v. Amnesty Int'l USA* (2013). In light of this "overriding and time-honored concern about keeping the Judiciary's power within its proper constitutional sphere, we must put aside the natural urge to proceed directly to the merits of [an] important dispute and to 'settle' it for the sake of convenience and efficiency." *Raines v. Byrd* (1997).

Most standing cases consider whether a plaintiff has satisfied the requirement when filing suit, but Article III demands that an "actual controversy" persist throughout all stages of litigation. *Already, LLC v. Nike, Inc.* (2013) (internal quotation marks omitted). That means that standing "must be met by persons seeking appellate review, just as it must be met by persons appearing in courts of first instance." *Arizonans for Official English v. Arizona* (1997). We therefore must decide whether petitioners had standing to appeal the District Court's order.

Respondents initiated this case in the District Court against the California officials responsible for enforcing Proposition 8. The parties do not contest that respondents had Article III standing to do so. Each couple expressed a desire to marry and obtain "official sanction" from the State, which was unavailable to them given the declaration in Proposition 8 that "marriage" in California is solely between a man and a woman.

After the District Court declared Proposition 8 unconstitutional and enjoined the state officials named as defendants from enforcing it, however, the inquiry under Article III changed. Respondents no longer had any injury to redress—they had won—and the state officials chose not to appeal.

The only individuals who sought to appeal that order were petitioners, who had intervened in the District Court. But the District Court had not ordered them to do or refrain from doing anything. To have standing, a litigant must seek relief for an injury that affects him in a "personal and individual way." *Defenders of Wildlife*. He must possess a "direct stake in the outcome" of the case. *Arizonans for Official English*. Here, however, petitioners had no "direct stake" in the outcome of their appeal. Their only interest in having the District Court order reversed was to vindicate the constitutional validity of a generally applicable California law.

We have repeatedly held that such a "generalized grievance," no matter how sincere, is insufficient to confer standing. A litigant "raising only a generally available grievance about government—claiming only harm to his and every citizen's interest in proper application of the Constitution and laws, and seeking relief that no more directly and tangibly benefits him than it does the public at large—does not state an Article III case or controversy." *Defenders of Wildlife.*

Petitioners argue that the California Constitution and its election laws give them a "'unique,' 'special,' and 'distinct' role in the initiative process—one 'involving both authority and responsibilities that differ from other supporters of the measure.'" True enough—but only when it comes to the process of enacting the law. Upon submitting the proposed initiative to the attorney general, petitioners became the official "proponents" of Proposition 8. As such, they were responsible for collecting the signatures required to qualify the measure for the ballot. After those signatures were collected, the proponents alone had the right to file the measure with election officials to put it on the ballot. Petitioners also possessed control over the arguments in favor of the initiative that would appear in California's ballot pamphlets.

But once Proposition 8 was approved by the voters, the measure became "a duly enacted constitutional amendment or statute." *Perry*. Petitioners have no role—special or otherwise—in the enforcement of Proposition 8. See *id.* (petitioners do not "possess any official authority . . . to directly enforce the initiative measure in question"). They therefore have no "personal stake" in defending its enforcement that is distinguishable from the general interest of every citizen of California. *Defenders of Wildlife*.

Article III standing "is not to be placed in the hands of 'concerned bystanders,' who will use it simply as a 'vehicle for the vindication of value interests.'" *Diamond*. No matter how deeply committed petitioners may be to upholding Proposition 8 or how "zealous [their] advocacy," (Kennedy, J., dissenting), that is not a "particularized" interest sufficient to create a case or controversy under Article III.

III

A

Without a judicially cognizable interest of their own, petitioners attempt to invoke that of someone else. They assert that even if *they* have no cognizable interest in appealing the District Court's judgment, the State of California does, and they may assert that interest on the State's behalf. It is, however, a "fundamental restriction on our authority" that "[i]n the ordinary course, a litigant must assert his or her own legal rights and interests, and cannot rest a claim to relief on the legal rights or interests of third parties." *Powers v. Ohio* (1991). There are "certain, limited exceptions" to that rule. But even when we have allowed litigants to assert the interests of others, the litigants themselves still "must have suffered an injury in fact, thus giving [them] a sufficiently concrete interest in the outcome of the issue in dispute." In *Diamond v. Charles,* for example, we refused to allow Diamond, a pediatrician engaged in private practice in Illinois, to defend the constitutionality of the State's abortion law. In that case, a group of physicians filed a constitutional challenge to the Illinois statute in federal court. The State initially defended the law, and Diamond, a professed "conscientious object[or] to abortions," intervened to defend it alongside the State.

After the Seventh Circuit affirmed a permanent injunction against enforcing several provisions of the law, the State chose not to pursue an appeal to this Court. But when Diamond did, the state attorney general filed a "letter of interest," explaining that the State's interest in the proceeding was "essentially coterminous with the position on the issues set forth by [Diamond]." That was not enough, we held, to allow the appeal to proceed. As the Court explained, "[e]ven if there were circumstances in which a private party would have standing to defend the constitutionality of a challenged statute, this [was] not one of them," because Diamond was not able to assert an injury in fact of his own. And without "any judicially cognizable interest," Diamond could not "maintain the litigation abandoned by the State."

For the reasons we have explained, petitioners have likewise not suffered an injury in fact, and therefore would ordinarily have no standing to assert the State's interests.

B

Petitioners contend that this case is different, because the California Supreme Court has determined that they are "authorized under California law to appear and assert the state's interest" in the validity of Proposition 8. The court below agreed: "All a federal court need determine is that the state has suffered a harm sufficient to confer standing and that the party seeking to invoke the jurisdiction of the court is authorized by the state to represent its interest in remedying that harm." As petitioners put it, they "need no more show a personal injury, separate from the State's indisputable interest in the validity of its law, than would California's Attorney General or did the legislative leaders held to have standing in *Karcher v. May* (1987)." In *Karcher,* we held that two New Jersey state legislators—Speaker of the General Assembly Alan Karcher and President of the Senate Carmen Orechio—could intervene in a suit against the State to defend the constitutionality of a New Jersey law, after the New Jersey attorney general had declined to do so. "Since the New Jersey Legislature had authority under state law to represent the State's interests in both the District Court and the Court of Appeals," we held that the Speaker and the President, in their official capacities, could vindicate that interest in federal court on the legislature's behalf.

Far from supporting petitioners' standing, however, *Karcher* is compelling precedent against it. The legislators in that case intervened in their official capacities as Speaker and President of the legislature. No one doubts that a State has a cognizable interest "in the continued enforceability" of its laws that is harmed by a judicial decision declaring a state law unconstitutional. To vindicate that interest or any other, a State must be able to designate agents to represent it in federal court. See *Poindexter v. Greenhow* (1885) ("The State is a political corporate body [that] can act only through agents"). That agent is typically the State's attorney general. But state law may provide for other officials to speak for the State in federal court, as New Jersey law did for the State's presiding legislative officers in *Karcher*.

What is significant about *Karcher* is what happened after the Court of Appeals decision in that case. Karcher and Orechio lost their positions as Speaker and President, but nevertheless sought to appeal to this Court. We held that they could not do so. We explained that while they were able to participate in the lawsuit in their official capacities as presiding officers of the incumbent legislature, "since they no longer hold those offices, they lack authority to pursue this appeal."

The point of *Karcher* is not that a State could authorize *private parties* to represent its interests; Karcher and Orechio were permitted to proceed only because they were state officers, acting in an official capacity. As soon as they lost that capacity, they lost standing. Petitioners here hold no office and have always participated in this litigation solely as private parties. . . .

C

Both petitioners and respondents seek support from dicta in *Arizonans for Official English v. Arizona*. The plaintiff in *Arizonans for Official English* filed a constitutional challenge to an Arizona ballot initiative declaring English "the official language of the State of Arizona." After the District Court declared the initiative unconstitutional, Arizona's Governor announced that she would not pursue an appeal. Instead, the principal sponsor of the ballot initiative—the Arizonans for Official English Committee—sought to defend the measure in the Ninth Circuit. Analogizing the sponsors to the Arizona Legislature, the Ninth Circuit held that the Committee was "qualified to defend [the initiative] on appeal," and affirmed the District Court. Before finding the case mooted by other events, this Court expressed "grave doubts" about the Ninth Circuit's standing analysis. We reiterated that "[s]tanding to defend on appeal in the place of an original defendant . . . demands that the litigant possess 'a direct stake in the outcome.'" (quoting *Diamond*). We recognized that a legislator authorized by state law to represent the State's interest may satisfy standing requirements, as in *Karcher*, but noted that the Arizona committee and its members were "not elected representatives, and we [we]re aware of no Arizona law appointing initiative sponsors as agents of the people of Arizona to defend, in lieu of public officials, the constitutionality of initiatives made law of the State." *Arizonans for Official English.*

Petitioners argue that, by virtue of the California Supreme Court's decision, they *are* authorized to act " 'as agents of the people' of California." But that Court never described petitioners as "agents of the people," or of anyone else. Nor did the Ninth Circuit. The Ninth Circuit asked—and the California Supreme Court answered—only whether petitioners had "the authority to assert the State's interest in the initiative's validity." All that the California Supreme Court decision stands for is that, so far as California is concerned, petitioners may argue in defense of Proposition 8. This "does not mean that the proponents become de facto public officials"; the authority they enjoy is "simply the authority to participate as parties in a court action and to assert legal arguments in defense of the state's interest in the validity of the initiative measure." That interest is by definition a generalized one, and it is precisely because proponents assert such an interest that they lack standing under our precedents.

And petitioners are plainly not agents of the State—"formal" or otherwise. . . . [T]he point, the most basic features of an agency relationship are missing here. Agency requires more than mere authorization to assert a particular interest. "An essential element of agency is the principal's right to control the agent's actions." 1 Restatement (Third) of Agency §1.01, Comment *f* (2005) (hereinafter Restatement). Yet petitioners answer to no one; they decide for themselves, with no review, what arguments to make and how to make them. Unlike California's attorney general, they are not elected at regular intervals—or elected at all. No provision provides for their removal. As one *amicus* explains, "the proponents apparently have an unelected appointment for an unspecified period of time as defenders of the initiative, however and to whatever extent they choose to defend it." Brief for Walter Dellinger. "If the relationship between two persons is one of agency . . . , the agent owes a fiduciary obligation to the principal." 1 Restatement §1.01, Comment *e*. But petitioners owe nothing of the sort to the people of California. Unlike California's elected officials, they have taken no oath of office. As the California Supreme Court explained, petitioners are bound simply by "the same ethical constraints that apply to all other parties in a legal proceeding." They are free to pursue a purely ideological commitment to the law's constitutionality without the need to take cognizance of resource constraints, changes in public opinion, or potential ramifications for other state priorities. . . .

Neither the California Supreme Court nor the Ninth Circuit ever described the proponents as agents of the State, and they plainly do not qualify as such.

IV

The dissent eloquently recounts the California Supreme Court's reasons for deciding that state law authorizes petitioners to defend Proposition 8. . . . We do not "disrespect[ ]" or "disparage[ ]" those reasons. Nor do we question California's sovereign right to maintain an initiative process, or the right of initiative proponents to defend their initiatives in California courts, where Article III does not apply. But as the dissent acknowledges, standing in federal court is a question of federal law, not state law. And no matter its reasons, the fact that a State thinks a private party should have standing to seek relief for a generalized grievance cannot override our settled law to the contrary. The Article III requirement that a party invoking the jurisdiction of a federal court seek relief for a personal, particularized injury serves vital interests going to the role of the Judiciary in our system of separated powers. "Refusing to entertain generalized grievances ensures that . . . courts exercise power that is judicial in nature," *Lance*, and ensures that the Federal Judiciary respects "the proper—and properly limited—role of the courts in a democratic society," *DaimlerChrysler Corp. v. Cuno* (2006). States cannot alter that role simply by issuing to private parties who otherwise lack standing a ticket to the federal courthouse.

* * *

We have never before upheld the standing of a private party to defend the constitutionality of a state statute when state officials have chosen not to. We decline to do so for the first time here. Because petitioners have not satisfied their burden to demonstrate standing to appeal the judgment of the District Court, the Ninth Circuit was without jurisdiction to consider the appeal. The judgment of the Ninth Circuit is vacated, and the case is remanded with instructions to dismiss the appeal for lack of jurisdiction. It is so ordered.

JUSTICE KENNEDY, with whom JUSTICE THOMAS, JUSTICE ALITO, and JUSTICE SOTOMAYOR join, dissenting. . . .

In my view Article III does not require California, when deciding who may appear in court to defend an initiative on its behalf, to comply with the Restatement of Agency or with this Court's view of how a State should make its laws or structure its government. The Court's reasoning does not take into account the fundamental principles or the practical dynamics of the initiative system in California, which uses this mechanism to control and to bypass public officials—the same officials who would not defend the initiative, an injury the Court now leaves unremedied. The Court's decision also has implications for the 26 other States that use an initiative or popular referendum system and which, like California, may choose to have initiative proponents stand in for the State when public officials decline to defend an initiative in litigation. In my submission, the Article III requirement for a justiciable case or controversy does not prevent proponents from having their day in court.

These are the premises for this respectful dissent.

I

As the Court explains, the State of California sustained a concrete injury, sufficient to satisfy the requirements of Article III, when a United States District Court nullified a portion of its State Constitution. To determine whether justiciability continues in appellate proceedings after the State Executive acquiesced in the District Court's adverse judgment, it is necessary to ascertain what persons, if any, have "authority under state law to represent the State's interests" in federal court. *Karcher v. May* (1987). . . .

This Court, in determining the substance of state law, is "bound by a state court's construction of a state statute." *Wisconsin v. Mitchell* (1993). And the Supreme Court of California, in response to the certified question submitted to it in this case, has determined that State Elections Code provisions directed to initiative proponents do inform and instruct state law respecting the rights and status of proponents in post election judicial proceedings. Here, in reliance on these statutes and the California Constitution, the State Supreme Court has held that proponents do have authority "under California law to appear and assert the state's interest in the initiative's validity and appeal a judgment invalidating the measure when the public officials who ordinarily defend the measure or appeal such a judgment decline to do so." *Perry v. Brown* (Cal. 2011).

The reasons the Supreme Court of California gave for its holding have special relevance in the context of determining whether proponents have the authority to seek a federal-court remedy for the State's concrete, substantial, and continuing injury. As a class, official proponents are a small, identifiable group. Because many of their decisions must be unanimous, they are necessarily few in number. Their identities are public. Their commitment is substantial [including obtaining petition signatures, paying monetary fee, and drafting arguments for official ballot pamphlet]. They know and understand the purpose and operation of the proposed law, an important requisite in defending initiatives on complex matters such as taxation and insurance. Having gone to great lengths to convince voters to enact an initiative, they have a stake in the outcome and the necessary commitment to provide zealous advocacy.

Thus, in California, proponents play a "unique role . . . in the initiative process." They "have a unique relationship to the voter-approved measure that makes them especially likely to be reliable and vigorous advocates for the measure and to be so viewed by those whose votes secured the initiative's enactment into law." See also *id.* (because of "their special relationship to the initiative measure," proponents are "the most obvious and logical private individuals to ably and vigorously defend the validity of the challenged measure on behalf of the interests of the voters who adopted the initiative into law"). Proponents' authority under state law is not a contrivance. It is not a fictional construct. It is the product of the California Constitution and the California Elections Code. There is no basis for this Court to set aside the California Supreme Court's determination of state law. . . .

For these and other reasons, the Supreme Court of California held that the California Elections Code and Article II, §8, of the California Constitution afford proponents "the authority . . . to assert the state's interest in the validity of the initiative" when State officials decline to do so. The court repeated this unanimous holding more than a half-dozen times and in no uncertain terms. That should suffice to resolve the central issue on which the federal question turns.

II

A

The Court concludes that proponents lack sufficient ties to the state government. It notes that they "are not elected," "answer to no one," and lack "a fiduciary obligation" to the State (quoting 1 Restatement (Third) of Agency §1.01, Comments *e, f* (2005)). But what the Court deems deficiencies in the proponents' connection to the State government, the State Supreme Court saw as essential qualifications to defend the initiative system. The very object of the initiative system is to establish a lawmaking process that does not depend upon state officials. In California, the popular initiative is necessary to implement "the theory that all power of government ultimately resides in the people." The right to adopt initiatives has been described by the California courts as "one of the most precious rights of [the State's] democratic process." That historic role for the initiative system "grew out of dissatisfaction with the then governing public officials and a widespread belief that the people had lost control of the political process." The initiative's "primary purpose," then, "was to afford the people the ability to propose and to adopt constitutional amendments or statutory provisions that their elected public officials had refused or declined to adopt." The California Supreme Court has determined that this purpose is undermined if the very officials the initiative process seeks to circumvent are the only parties who can defend an enacted initiative when it is challenged in a legal proceeding. Giving the Governor and attorney general this *de facto* veto will erode one of the cornerstones of the State's governmental structure. And in light of the frequency with which initiatives' opponents resort to litigation, the impact of that veto could be substantial. As a consequence, California finds it necessary to vest the responsibility and right to defend a voter-approved initiative in the initiative's proponents when the State Executive declines to do so.

Yet today the Court demands that the State follow the Restatement of Agency. There are reasons, however, why California might conclude that a conventional agency relationship is inconsistent with the history, design, and purpose of the initiative process. The State may not wish to associate itself with proponents or their views outside of the "extremely narrow and limited" context of this litigation, or to bear the cost of proponents' legal fees. The State may also wish to avoid the odd conflict of having a formal agent of the State (the initiative's proponent) arguing in favor of a law's validity while state officials (*e.g.*, the attorney general) contend in the same proceeding that it should be found invalid.

Furthermore, it is not clear who the principal in an agency relationship would be. It would make little sense if it were the Governor or attorney general, for that would frustrate the initiative system's purpose of circumventing elected officials who fail or refuse to effect the public will. If there is to be a principal, then, it must be the people of California, as the ultimate sovereign in the State. See [Cal. Const., Art. II, §1] ("All political power is inherent in the people.") But the Restatement may offer no workable example of an agent representing a principal composed of nearly 40 million residents of a State. Cf. 1 Restatement (Second) of Agency, p. 2, Scope Note (1957) (noting that the Restatement "does not state the special rules applicable to public officers").

And if the Court's concern is that the proponents are unaccountable, that fear is neither well founded nor sufficient to overcome the contrary judgment of the State Supreme Court. It must be remembered that both elected officials and initiative proponents receive their authority to speak for the State of California directly from the people. The Court apparently believes that elected officials are acceptable "agents" of the State, but they are no more subject to ongoing supervision of their principal—*i.e.,* the people of the State—than are initiative proponents. At most, a Governor or attorney general can be recalled or voted out of office in a subsequent election, but proponents, too, can have their authority terminated or their initiative overridden by a subsequent ballot measure. Finally, proponents and their attorneys, like all other litigants and counsel who appear before a federal court, are subject to duties of candor, decorum, and respect for the tribunal and co-parties alike, all of which guard against the possibility that initiative proponents will somehow fall short of the appropriate standards for federal litigation.

### B

Contrary to the Court's suggestion, this Court's precedents do not indicate that a formal agency relationship is necessary. In *Karcher v. May* (1987), the Speaker of the New Jersey Assembly (Karcher) and President of the New Jersey Senate (Orechio) intervened in support of a school moment-of-silence law that the State's Governor and attorney general declined to defend in court. In considering the question of standing, the Court looked to New Jersey law to determine whether Karcher and Orechio "had authority under state law to represent the State's interest in both the District Court and Court of Appeals." The Court concluded that they did. Because the "New Jersey Supreme Court ha[d] granted applications of the Speaker of the General Assembly and the President of the Senate to intervene as parties-respondent on behalf of the legislature in defense of a legislative enactment," the *Karcher* Court held that standing had been proper in the District Court and Court of Appeals. By the time the case arrived in this Court, Karcher and Orechio had lost their presiding legislative offices, without which they lacked the authority to represent the State under New Jersey law. This, the Court held, deprived them of standing. Here, by contrast, proponents' authority under California law is not contingent on officeholder status, so their standing is unaffected by the fact that they "hold no office" in California's Government. *Arizonans for Official English v. Arizona* (1997) is consistent with the premises of this dissent, not with the rationale of the Court's opinion. There, the Court noted its serious doubts as to the aspiring defenders' standing because there was "no Arizona law appointing initiative sponsors as agents of the people of Arizona to defend, in lieu of public officials, the constitutionality of initiatives made law of the State." The Court did use the word "agents"; but, read in context, it is evident that the Court's intention was not to demand a formal agency relationship in compliance with the Restatement. Rather, the Court used the term as shorthand for a party whom "state law authorizes" to "represent the State's interests" in court. . . .

### III

There is much irony in the Court's approach to justiciability in this case. A prime purpose of justiciability is to ensure vigorous advocacy, yet the Court insists upon litigation conducted by state officials whose preference is to lose the case. The doctrine is meant to ensure that courts are responsible and constrained in their power, but the Court's opinion today means that a single district court can make a decision with far-reaching effects that cannot be reviewed. And rather than honor the principle that justiciability exists to allow disputes of public policy to be resolved by the political process rather than the courts, see, *e.g., Allen v. Wright* (1984), here the Court refuses to allow a State's authorized representatives to defend the outcome of a democratic election. The Court's opinion disrespects and disparages both the political process in California and the well-stated opinion of the California Supreme Court in this case. The California Supreme Court, not this Court, expresses concern for vigorous representation; the California Supreme Court, not this Court, recognizes the necessity to avoid conflicts of interest; the California Supreme Court, not this Court, comprehends the real interest at stake in this litigation and identifies the most proper party to defend that interest. The California Supreme Court's opinion reflects a better understanding of the dynamics and principles of Article III than does this Court's opinion. . . .

* * *

In the end, what the Court fails to grasp or accept is the basic premise of the initiative process. And it is this. The essence of democracy is that the right to make law rests in the people and flows to the government, not the other way around. Freedom resides first in the people without need of a grant from government.

The California initiative process embodies these principles and has done so for over a century. . . . In California and the 26 other States that permit initiatives and popular referendums, the people have exercised their own inherent sovereign right to govern themselves. The Court today frustrates that choice by nullifying, for failure to comply with the Restatement of Agency, a State Supreme Court decision holding that state law authorizes an enacted initiative's proponents to defend the law if and when the State's usual legal advocates decline to do so. The Court's opinion fails to abide by precedent and misapplies basic principles of justiciability. Those errors necessitate this respectful dissent.

# *Chapter 4*

# *The Equal Protection of the Law: Racial Discrimination*

## *ASSIGNMENT S-5*

### "Reverse" Racial Discrimination

### Admission to School

FISHER v. UNIVERSITY OF TEXAS AT AUSTIN

*No. 11-345. | Decided June 24, 2013*

KENNEDY, J., delivered the opinion of the Court, in which ROBERTS, C.J., and SCALIA, THOMAS, BREYER, ALITO, and SOTOMAYOR, JJ., joined. SCALIA, J., and THOMAS, J., filed concurring opinions. GINSBURG, J., filed a dissenting opinion. KAGAN, J., took no part in the consideration or decision of the case.

JUSTICE KENNEDY delivered the opinion of the Court.

The University of Texas at Austin considers race as one of various factors in its undergraduate admissions process. Race is not itself assigned a numerical value for each applicant, but the University has committed itself to increasing racial minority enrollment on campus. It refers to this goal as a "critical mass." Petitioner, who is Caucasian, sued the University after her application was rejected. She contends that the University's use of race in the admissions process violated the Equal Protection Clause of the Fourteenth Amendment.

The parties asked the Court to review whether the judgment below was consistent with "this Court's decisions interpreting the Equal Protection Clause of the Fourteenth Amendment, including Grutter v. Bollinger (2003)." Pet. for Cert. i. The Court concludes that the Court of Appeals did not hold the University to the demanding burden of strict scrutiny articulated in *Grutter* and *Regents of Univ. of Cal. v. Bakke* (1978) (opinion of Powell, J.). Because the Court of Appeals did not apply the correct standard of strict scrutiny, its decision affirming the District Court's grant of summary judgment to the University was incorrect. That decision is vacated, and the case is remanded for further proceedings.

I

A

Located in Austin, Texas, on the most renowned campus of the Texas state university system, the University is one of the leading institutions of higher education in the Nation. Admission is prized and competitive. In 2008, when petitioner sought admission to the University's entering class, she was 1 of 29,501 applicants. From this group 12,843 were admitted, and 6,715 accepted and enrolled. Petitioner was denied admission.

In recent years the University has used three different programs to evaluate candidates for admission. The first is the program it used for some years before 1997, when the University considered two factors: a numerical score reflecting an applicant's test scores and academic performance in high school (Academic Index or AI), and the applicant's race. In 1996, this system was held unconstitutional by the United States Court of Appeals for the Fifth Circuit. It ruled the University's consideration of race violated the Equal Protection Clause because it did not further any compelling government interest. *Hopwood v. Texas* (1996).

The second program was adopted to comply with the *Hopwood* decision. The University stopped considering race in admissions and substituted instead a new holistic metric of a candidate's potential contribution to the University, to be used in conjunction with the Academic Index. This "Personal Achievement Index" (PAI) measures a student's leadership and work experience, awards, extracurricular activities, community service, and other special circumstances that give insight into a student's background. These included growing up in a single-parent home, speaking a language other than English at home, significant family responsibilities assumed by the applicant, and the general socioeconomic condition of the student's family. Seeking to address the decline in minority enrollment after *Hopwood*, the University also expanded its outreach programs.

The Texas State Legislature also responded to the *Hopwood* decision. It enacted a measure known as the Top Ten Percent Law (West 2009). Also referred to as H. B. 588, the Top Ten Percent Law grants automatic admission to any public state college, including the University, to all students in the top 10% of their class at high schools in Texas that comply with certain standards.

The University's revised admissions process, coupled with the operation of the Top Ten Percent Law, resulted in a more racially diverse environment at the University. Before the admissions program at issue in this case, in the last year under the post-*Hopwood* AI/PAI system that did not consider race, the entering class was 4.5% African-American and 16.9% Hispanic. This is in contrast with the 1996 pre-*Hopwood* and Top Ten Percent regime, when race was explicitly considered, and the University's entering freshman class was 4.1% African-American and 14.5% Hispanic.

Following this Court's decisions in *Grutter v. Bollinger* and *Gratz v. Bollinger* (2003), the University adopted a third admissions program, the 2004 program in which the University reverted to explicit consideration of race. This is the program here at issue. In *Grutter*, the Court upheld the use of race as one of many "plus factors" in an admissions program that considered the overall individual contribution of each candidate. In *Gratz*, by contrast, the Court held unconstitutional Michigan's undergraduate admissions program, which automatically awarded points to applicants from certain racial minorities.

The University's plan to resume race-conscious admissions was given formal expression in June 2004 in an internal document entitled *Proposal to Consider Race and Ethnicity in Admissions* (Proposal). The Proposal relied in substantial part on a study of a subset of undergraduate classes containing between 5 and 24 students. It showed that few of these classes had significant enrollment by members of racial minorities. In addition the Proposal relied on what it called "anecdotal" reports from students regarding their "interaction in the classroom." The Proposal concluded that the University lacked a "critical mass" of minority students and that to remedy the deficiency it was necessary to give explicit consideration to race in the undergraduate admissions program.

To implement the Proposal the University included a student's race as a component of the PAI score, beginning with applicants in the fall of 2004. The University asks students to classify themselves from among five predefined racial categories on the application. Race is not assigned an explicit numerical value, but it is undisputed that race is a meaningful factor.

Once applications have been scored, they are plotted on a grid with the Academic Index on the x-axis and the Personal Achievement Index on the y-axis. On that grid students are assigned to so-called cells based on their individual scores. All students in the cells falling above a certain line are admitted. All students below the line are not. Each college—such as Liberal Arts or Engineering—admits students separately. So a student is considered initially for her first-choice college, then for her second choice, and finally for general admission as an undeclared major. . . .

The District Court granted summary judgment to the University. The United States Court of Appeals for the Fifth Circuit affirmed. It held that *Grutter* required courts to give substantial deference to the University, both in the definition of the compelling interest in diversity's benefits and in deciding whether its specific plan was narrowly tailored to achieve its stated goal. Applying that standard, the court upheld the University's admissions plan. . . .

B

Among the Court's cases involving racial classifications in education, there are three decisions that directly address the question of considering racial minority status as a positive or favorable factor in a university's admissions process, with the goal of achieving the educational benefits of a more diverse student body: *Bakke*, *Gratz*, and *Grutter*. We take those cases as given for purposes of deciding this case. We begin with the principal opinion authored by Justice Powell in *Bakke*. In *Bakke*, the Court considered a system used by the medical school of the University of California at Davis. From an entering class of 100 students the school had set aside 16 seats for minority applicants. In holding this program impermissible under the Equal Protection Clause Justice Powell's opinion stated certain basic premises. First, "decisions based on race or ethnic origin by faculties and administrations of state universities are reviewable under the Fourteenth Amendment." The principle of equal protection admits no "artificial line of a 'two-class theory'" that "permits the recognition of special wards entitled to a degree of protection greater than that accorded others." It is therefore irrelevant that a system of racial preferences in admissions may seem benign. Any racial classification must meet strict scrutiny, for when government decisions "touch upon an individual's race or ethnic background, he is entitled to a judicial determination that the burden he is asked to bear on that basis is precisely tailored to serve a compelling governmental interest."

Next, Justice Powell identified one compelling interest that could justify the consideration of race: the interest in the educational benefits that flow from a diverse student body. Redressing past discrimination could not serve as a compelling interest, because a university's "broad mission [of] education" is incompatible with making the "judicial, legislative, or administrative findings of constitutional or statutory violations" necessary to justify remedial racial classification.

The attainment of a diverse student body, by contrast, serves values beyond race alone, including enhanced classroom dialogue and the lessening of racial isolation and stereotypes. . . . Justice Powell's central point, however, was that this interest in securing diversity's benefits, although a permissible objective, is complex. "It is not an interest in simple ethnic diversity, in which a specified percentage of the student body is in effect guaranteed to be members of selected ethnic groups, with the remaining percentage an undifferentiated aggregation of students. The diversity that furthers a compelling state interest encompasses a far broader array of qualifications and characteristics of which racial or ethnic origin is but a single though important element."

In *Gratz* and *Grutter*, the Court endorsed the precepts stated by Justice Powell. In *Grutter*, the Court reaffirmed his conclusion that obtaining the educational benefits of "student body diversity is a compelling state interest that can justify the use of race in university admissions."

As *Gratz* and *Grutter* observed, however, this follows only if a clear precondition is met: The particular admissions process used for this objective is subject to judicial review. Race may not be considered unless the admissions process can withstand strict scrutiny. "Nothing in Justice Powell's opinion in *Bakke* signaled that a university may employ whatever means it desires to achieve the stated goal of diversity without regard to the limits imposed by our strict scrutiny analysis." *Gratz*. "To be narrowly tailored, a race-conscious admissions program cannot use a quota system," *Grutter*, but instead must "remain flexible enough to ensure that each applicant is evaluated as an individual and not in a way that makes an applicant's race or ethnicity the defining feature of his or her application." Strict scrutiny requires the university to demonstrate with clarity that its "purpose or interest is both constitutionally permissible and substantial, and that its use of the classification is necessary . . . to the accomplishment of its purpose." *Bakke* (opinion of Powell, J.).

While these are the cases that most specifically address the central issue in this case, additional guidance may be found in the Court's broader equal protection jurisprudence which applies in this context. "Distinctions between citizens solely because of their ancestry are by their very nature odious to a free people," *Rice v. Cayetano* (2000) (internal quotation marks omitted), and therefore "are contrary to our traditions and hence constitutionally suspect," *Bolling v. Sharpe* (1954). " '[B]ecause racial characteristics so seldom provide a relevant basis for disparate treatment,' " *Richmond v. J. A. Croson Co.* (1989), "the Equal Protection Clause demands that racial classifications . . . be subjected to the 'most rigid scrutiny.' " *Loving v. Virginia* (1967).

To implement these canons, judicial review must begin from the position that "any official action that treats a person differently on account of his race or ethnic origin is inherently suspect." *Fullilove* [*v. Klutznick* (1980)] (Stewart, J., dissenting). Strict scrutiny is a searching examination, and it is the government that bears the burden to prove " 'that the reasons for any [racial] classification [are] clearly identified and unquestionably legitimate,' " *Croson*.

II

*Grutter* made clear that racial "classifications are constitutional only if they are narrowly tailored to further compelling governmental interests." And *Grutter* endorsed Justice Powell's conclusion in *Bakke* that "the attainment of a diverse student body . . . is a constitutionally permissible goal for an institution of higher education." Thus, under *Grutter*, strict scrutiny must be applied to any admissions program using racial categories or classifications.

According to *Grutter*, a university's "educational judgment that such diversity is essential to its educational mission is one to which we defer." *Grutter* concluded that the decision to pursue "the educational benefits that flow from student body diversity," that the University deems integral to its mission is, in substantial measure, an academic judgment to which some, but not complete, judicial deference is proper under *Grutter*. A court, of course, should ensure that there is a reasoned, principled explanation for the academic decision. On this point, the District Court and Court of Appeals were correct in finding that *Grutter* calls for deference to the University's conclusion, " 'based on its experience and expertise,' " that a diverse student body would serve its educational goals. There is disagreement about whether *Grutter* was consistent with the principles of equal protection in approving this compelling interest in diversity. But the parties here do not ask the Court to revisit that aspect of *Grutter*'s holding.

A university is not permitted to define diversity as "some specified percentage of a particular group merely because of its race or ethnic origin." *Bakke*, "That would amount to outright racial balancing, which is patently unconstitutional." *Grutter*. "Racial balancing is not transformed from 'patently unconstitutional' to a compelling state interest simply by relabeling it 'racial diversity.' " *Parents Involved in Community Schools v. Seattle School Dist. No. 1* (2007).

Once the University has established that its goal of diversity is consistent with strict scrutiny, however, there must still be a further judicial determination that the admissions process meets strict scrutiny in its implementation. The University must prove that the means chosen by the University to attain diversity are narrowly tailored to that goal. On this point, the University receives no deference. *Grutter* made clear that it is for the courts, not for university administrators, to ensure that "[t]he means chosen to accomplish the [government's] asserted purpose must be specifically and narrowly framed to accomplish that purpose." True, a court can take account of a university's experience and expertise in adopting or rejecting certain admissions processes. But, as the Court said in *Grutter*, it remains at all times the University's obligation to demonstrate, and the Judiciary's obligation to determine, that admissions processes "ensure that each applicant is evaluated as an individual and not in a way that makes an applicant's race or ethnicity the defining feature of his or her application."

Narrow tailoring also requires that the reviewing court verify that it is "necessary" for a university to use race to achieve the educational benefits of diversity. *Bakke*. This involves a careful judicial inquiry into whether a university could achieve sufficient diversity without using racial classifications. Although "[n]arrow tailoring does not require exhaustion of every *conceivable* race-neutral alternative," strict scrutiny does require a court to examine with care, and not defer to, a university's "serious, good faith consideration of workable race-neutral alternatives." See *Grutter* (emphasis added). Consideration by the university is of course necessary, but it is not sufficient to satisfy strict scrutiny: The reviewing court must ultimately be satisfied that no workable race-neutral alternatives would produce the educational benefits of diversity. If " 'a nonracial approach . . . could promote the substantial interest about as well and at tolerable administrative expense,' " *Wygant v. Jackson Bd. of Ed.* (1986) (quoting Greenawalt, Judicial Scrutiny of "Benign" Racial Preference in Law School Admissions, 75 Colum. L. Rev. 559, 578-579 (1975)), then the university may not consider race. A plaintiff, of course, bears the burden of placing the validity of a university's adoption of an affirmative action plan in issue. But strict scrutiny imposes on the university the ultimate burden of demonstrating, before turning to racial classifications, that available, workable race-neutral alternatives do not suffice.

Rather than perform this searching examination, however, the Court of Appeals held petitioner could challenge only "whether [the University's] decision to reintroduce race as a factor in admissions was made in good faith." And in considering such a challenge, the court would "presume the University acted in good faith" and place on petitioner the burden of rebutting that presumption. The Court of Appeals held that to "second-guess the merits" of this aspect of the University's decision was a task it was "ill-equipped to perform" and that it would attempt only to "ensure that [the University's] decision to adopt a race-conscious admissions policy followed from [a process of] good faith consideration." The Court of Appeals thus concluded that "the narrow-tailoring inquiry—like the compelling-interest inquiry—is undertaken with a degree of deference to the Universit[y]." Because "the efforts of the University have been studied, serious, and of high purpose," the Court of Appeals held that the use of race in the admissions program fell within "a constitutionally protected zone of discretion."

These expressions of the controlling standard are at odds with *Grutter*'s command that "all racial classifications imposed by government 'must be analyzed by a reviewing court under strict scrutiny.' " (quoting *Adarand Constructors, Inc. v. Peña* (1995)). In *Grutter*, the Court approved the plan at issue upon concluding that it was not a quota, was sufficiently flexible, was limited in time, and followed "serious, good faith consideration of workable race-neutral alternatives." As noted above, the parties do not challenge, and the Court therefore does not consider, the correctness of that determination.

*Grutter* did not hold that good faith would forgive an impermissible consideration of race. It must be remembered that "the mere recitation of a 'benign' or legitimate purpose for a racial classification is entitled to little or no weight." *Croson*. Strict scrutiny does not permit a court to accept a school's assertion that its admissions process uses race in a permissible way without a court giving close analysis to the evidence of how the process works in practice.

The higher education dynamic does not change the narrow tailoring analysis of strict scrutiny applicable in other contexts. . . . The District Court and Court of Appeals confined the strict scrutiny inquiry in too narrow a way by deferring to the University's good faith in its use of racial classifications and affirming the grant of summary judgment on that basis. The Court vacates that judgment, but fairness to the litigants and the courts that heard the case requires that it be remanded so that the admissions process can be considered and judged under a correct analysis. Unlike *Grutter*, which was decided after trial, this case arises from cross-motions for summary judgment. In this case, as in similar cases, in determining whether summary judgment in favor of the University would be appropriate, the Court of Appeals must assess whether the University has offered sufficient evidence that would prove that its admissions program is narrowly tailored to obtain the educational benefits of diversity. Whether this record—and not "simple . . . assurances of good intention," *Croson*—is sufficient is a question for the Court of Appeals in the first instance.

* * *

Strict scrutiny must not be " 'strict in theory, but fatal in fact,' " *Adarand*. But the opposite is also true. Strict scrutiny must not be strict in theory but feeble in fact. In order for judicial review to be meaningful, a university must make a showing that its plan is narrowly tailored to achieve the only interest that this Court has approved in this context: the benefits of a student body diversity that "encompasses a . . . broa[d] array of qualifications and characteristics of which racial or ethnic origin is but a single though important element." *Bakke*. The judgment of the Court of Appeals is vacated, and the case is remanded for further proceedings consistent with this opinion.

It is so ordered.

JUSTICE KAGAN took no part in the consideration or decision of this case.

JUSTICE SCALIA, concurring.

I adhere to the view I expressed in *Grutter v. Bollinger*: "The Constitution proscribes government discrimination on the basis of race, and state-provided education is no exception." (opinion concurring in part and dissenting in part). The petitioner in this case did not ask us to overrule *Grutter*'s holding that a "compelling interest" in the educational benefits of diversity can justify racial preferences in university admissions. I therefore join the Court's opinion in full.

JUSTICE THOMAS, concurring.

I join the Court's opinion because I agree that the Court of Appeals did not apply strict scrutiny to the University of Texas at Austin's (University) use of racial discrimination in admissions decisions. I write separately to explain that I would overrule *Grutter v. Bollinger* (2003), and hold that a State's use of race in higher education admissions decisions is categorically prohibited by the Equal Protection Clause. . . .

I

A

The Fourteenth Amendment provides that no State shall "deny to any person . . . the equal protection of the laws." The Equal Protection Clause guarantees every person the right to be treated equally by the State, without regard to race. "At the heart of this [guarantee] lies the principle that the government must treat citizens as individuals, and not as members of racial, ethnic, or religious groups." *Missouri v. Jenkins* (1995) (Thomas, J., concurring). "It is for this reason that we must subject all racial classifications to the strictest of scrutiny." *Id.*, at 121.

Under strict scrutiny, all racial classifications are categorically prohibited unless they are " 'necessary to further a compelling governmental interest' " and "narrowly tailored to that end." *Johnson v. California* (2005) (quoting *Grutter*). This most exacting standard "has proven automatically fatal" in almost every case. *Jenkins* (Thomas, J., concurring). And rightly so. "Purchased at the price of immeasurable human suffering, the equal protection principle reflects our Nation's understanding that [racial] classifications ultimately have a destructive impact on the individual and our society." *Adarand Constructors, Inc. v. Peña* (1995) (Thomas, J., concurring in part and concurring in judgment). "The Constitution abhors classifications based on race" because "every time the government places citizens on racial registers and makes race relevant to the provision of burdens or benefits, it demeans us all." *Grutter* (Thomas, J., concurring in part and dissenting in part). . . .

B

2

*Grutter* was a radical departure from our strict-scrutiny precedents. In *Grutter*, the University of Michigan Law School (Law School) claimed that it had a compelling reason to discriminate based on race. The reason it advanced did not concern protecting national security or remedying its own past discrimination. Instead, the Law School argued that it needed to discriminate in admissions decisions in order to obtain the "educational benefits that flow from a diverse student body." Contrary to the very meaning of strict scrutiny, the Court deferred to the Law School's determination that this interest was sufficiently compelling to justify racial discrimination. I dissented from that part of the Court's decision. I explained that "only those measures the State must take to provide a bulwark against anarchy, or to prevent violence, will constitute a 'pressing public necessity'" sufficient to satisfy strict scrutiny. I adhere to that view today. As should be obvious, there is nothing "pressing" or "necessary" about obtaining whatever educational benefits may flow from racial diversity. . . .

III

While I find the theory advanced by the University to justify racial discrimination facially inadequate, I also believe that its use of race has little to do with the alleged educational benefits of diversity. I suspect that the University's program is instead based on the benighted notion that it is possible to tell when discrimination helps, rather than hurts, racial minorities. See post, at 3 (Ginsburg, J., dissenting) ("[G]overnment actors, including state universities, need not be blind to the lingering effects of 'an overtly discriminatory past,' the legacy of 'centuries of law-sanctioned inequality'"). But "[h]istory should teach greater humility." *Metro Broadcasting, Inc. v. FCC* (1990) (O'Connor, J., dissenting). The worst forms of racial discrimination in this Nation have always been accompanied by straight-faced representations that discrimination helped minorities.

A

Slaveholders argued that slavery was a "positive good" that civilized blacks and elevated them in every dimension of life. See, e.g., Calhoun, Speech in the U.S. Senate, 1837, in P. Finkelman, *Defending Slavery* (2003) ("Never before has the black race of Central Africa, from the dawn of history to the present day, attained a condition so civilized and so improved, not only physically, but morally and intellectually. . . . [T]he relation now existing in the slaveholding States between the two [races], is, instead of an evil, a good—a positive good"); Harper, Memoir on Slavery, in The Ideology of Slavery (D. Faust ed. 1981) ("Slavery, as it is said in an eloquent article published in a Southern periodical work . . . 'has done more to elevate a degraded race in the scale of humanity; to tame the savage; to civilize the barbarous; to soften the ferocious; to enlighten the ignorant, and to spread the blessings of [C]hristianity among the heathen, than all the missionaries that philanthropy and religion have ever sent forth'"); Hammond, The Mudsill Speech, 1858, in Defending Slavery ("They are elevated from the condition in which God first created them, by being made our slaves").

A century later, segregationists similarly asserted that segregation was not only benign, but good for black students. They argued, for example, that separate schools protected black children from racist white students and teachers. See, e.g., Brief for Appellees in *Briggs* ("'I have repeatedly seen wise and loving colored parents take infinite pains to force their little children into schools where the white children, white teachers, and white parents despised and resented the dark child, made mock of it, neglected or bullied it, and literally rendered its life a living hell. Such parents want their child to "fight" this thing out,—but, dear God, at what a cost! . . . We shall get a finer, better balance of spirit; an infinitely more capable and rounded personality by putting children in schools where they are wanted, and where they are happy and inspired, than in thrusting them into hells where they are ridiculed and hated'" (quoting DuBois, Does the Negro Need Separate Schools? 4 J. of Negro Educ. 328 (1935))); Tr. of Oral Arg. in *Bolling v. Sharpe*, 1952 ("There was behind these [a]cts a kindly feeling [and] an intention to help these people who had been in bondage. And there was and there still is an intention by the Congress to see that these children shall be educated in a healthful atmosphere, in a wholesome atmosphere, in a place where they are wanted, in a place where they will not be looked upon with hostility, in a place where there will be a receptive atmosphere for learning for both races without the hostility that undoubtedly Congress thought might creep into these situations"). And they even appealed to the fact that many blacks agreed that separate schools were in the "best interests" of both races. See, e.g., Brief for Appellees in *Davis* ("'It has been my experience, in working with the people of Virginia, including both white and Negro, that the customs and the habits and the traditions of Virginia citizens are such that they believe for the best interests of both the white and the Negro that the separate school is best'").

Following in these inauspicious footsteps, the University would have us believe that its discrimination is likewise benign. I think the lesson of history is clear enough: Racial discrimination is never benign. "'[B]enign' carries with it no independent meaning, but reflects only acceptance of the current generation's conclusion that a politically acceptable burden, imposed on particular citizens on the basis of race, is reasonable." See *Metro Broadcasting* (O'Connor, J., dissenting). It is for this reason that the Court has repeatedly held that strict scrutiny applies to all racial classifications, regardless of whether the government has benevolent motives. The University's professed good intentions cannot excuse its outright racial discrimination any more than such intentions justified the now denounced arguments of slaveholders and segregationists.

B

While it does not, for constitutional purposes, matter whether the University's racial discrimination is benign, I note that racial engineering does in fact have insidious consequences. There can be no doubt that the University's discrimination injures white and Asian applicants who are denied admission because of their race. But I believe the injury to those admitted under the University's discriminatory admissions program is even more harmful. Blacks and Hispanics admitted to the University as a result of racial discrimination are, on average, far less prepared than their white and Asian classmates. In the University's entering class of 2009, for example, among the students admitted outside the Top Ten Percent plan, blacks scored at the 52d percentile of 2009 SAT takers nationwide, while Asians scored at the 93d percentile. Brief for Richard Sander et al. as Amici Curiae 3-4, and n. 4. Blacks had a mean GPA of 2.57 and a mean SAT score of 1524; Hispanics had a mean GPA of 2.83 and a mean SAT score of 1794; whites had a mean GPA of 3.04 and a mean SAT score of 1914; and Asians had a mean GPA of 3.07 and a mean SAT score of 1991.[1]

Tellingly, neither the University nor any of the 73 amici briefs in support of racial discrimination has presented a shred of evidence that black and Hispanic students are able to close this substantial gap during their time at the University. There is no reason to believe this is not the case at the University. The University and its dozens of amici are deafeningly silent on this point.

Furthermore, the University's discrimination does nothing to increase the number of blacks and Hispanics who have access to a college education generally. Instead, the University's discrimination has a pervasive shifting effect. See T. Sowell, Affirmative Action Around the World 145-146 (2004). The University admits minorities who otherwise would have attended less selective colleges where they would have been more evenly matched. But, as a result of the mismatching, many blacks and Hispanics who likely would have excelled at less elite schools are placed in a position where underperformance is all but inevitable because they are less academically prepared than the white and Asian students with whom they must compete. Setting aside the damage wreaked upon the self confidence of these overmatched students, there is no evidence that they learn more at the University than they would have learned at other schools for which they were better prepared. Indeed, they may learn less. . . .

Moreover, the University's discrimination "stamp[s] [blacks and Hispanics] with a badge of inferiority." *Adarand* (opinion of Thomas, J.). It taints the accomplishments of all those who are admitted as a result of racial discrimination. Cf. J. McWhorter, Losing the Race: Self-Sabotage in Black America 248 (2000) ("I was never able to be as proud of getting into Stanford as my classmates could be. . . . [H]ow much of an achievement can I truly say it was to have been a good enough black person to be admitted, while my colleagues had been considered good enough people to be admitted"). And, it taints the accomplishments of all those who are the same race as those admitted as a result of racial discrimination. In this case, for example, most blacks and Hispanics attending the University were admitted without discrimination under the Top Ten Percent plan, but no one can distinguish those students from the ones whose race played a role in their admission. "When blacks [and Hispanics] take positions in the highest places of government, industry, or academia, it is an open question . . . whether their skin color played a part in their advancement." See *Grutter* (opinion of Thomas, J.). "The question itself is the stigma—because either racial discrimination did play a role, in which case the person may be deemed 'otherwise unqualified,' or it did not, in which case asking the question itself unfairly marks those . . . who would succeed without discrimination." Ibid. Although cloaked in good intentions, the University's racial tinkering harms the very people it claims to be helping.

* * *

1. The lowest possible score on the SAT is 600, and the highest possible score is 2400.

For the foregoing reasons, I would overrule *Grutter*. However, because the Court correctly concludes that the Court of Appeals did not apply strict scrutiny, I join its opinion.

JUSTICE GINSBURG, dissenting.

The University of Texas at Austin (University) is candid about what it is endeavoring to do: It seeks to achieve student-body diversity through an admissions policy patterned after the Harvard plan referenced as exemplary in Justice Powell's opinion in *Regents of Univ. of Cal. v. Bakke* (1978). The University has steered clear of a quota system like the one struck down in *Bakke*, which excluded all nonminority candidates from competition for a fixed number of seats. And, like so many educational institutions across the Nation, the University has taken care to follow the model approved by the Court in *Grutter v. Bollinger* (2003).

Texas' percentage plan was adopted with racially segregated neighborhoods and schools front and center stage. It is race consciousness, not blindness to race, that drives such plans. As for holistic review, if universities cannot explicitly include race as a factor, many may "resort to camouflage" to "maintain their minority enrollment." *Gratz* (Ginsburg, J., dissenting). I have several times explained why government actors, including state universities, need not be blind to the lingering effects of "an overtly discriminatory past," the legacy of "centuries of law-sanctioned inequality." *Id.* (dissenting opinion). Among constitutionally permissible options, I remain convinced, "those that candidly disclose their consideration of race [are] preferable to those that conceal it." *Gratz* (dissenting opinion).

Accordingly, I would not return this case for a second look. As the thorough opinions below show, the University's admissions policy flexibly considers race only as a "factor of a factor of a factor of a factor" in the calculus; followed a year long review through which the University reached the reasonable, good-faith judgment that supposedly race-neutral initiatives were insufficient to achieve, in appropriate measure, the educational benefits of student body diversity; and is subject to periodic review to ensure that the consideration of race remains necessary and proper to achieve the University's educational objectives. Justice Powell's opinion in *Bakke* and the Court's decision in *Grutter* require no further determinations.

The Court rightly declines to cast off the equal protection framework settled in *Grutter*. Yet it stops short of reaching the conclusion that framework warrants. Instead, the Court vacates the Court of Appeals' judgment and remands for the Court of Appeals to "assess whether the University has offered sufficient evidence [to] prove that its admissions program is narrowly tailored to obtain the educational benefits of diversity." *Ante*. As I see it, the Court of Appeals has already completed that inquiry, and its judgment, trained on this Court's *Bakke* and *Grutter* pathmarkers, merits our approbation.

For the reasons stated, I would affirm the judgment of the Court of Appeals.

# Chapter 5

# Modern Substantive Due Process

## ASSIGNMENT S-6

### Protecting "Liberty"

*Study Guide:*

- If, as Justice Kennedy wrote, "it is unnecessary to decide whether this federal intrusion on state power is a violation of the Constitution because it disrupts the federal balance," why does he persist in discussing such federalism issues throughout his opinion?
- How does the federal government defining marriage *for purposes of its own laws* interfere with, or infringe upon, the states' traditional power to define marriage?
- Can you articulate the *structure* of Justice Kennedy's analysis? How does it compare with the doctrines governing equal protection and due process described in the cases we have read? In particular, what does he say justifies heightened scrutiny in this case? (Hint: How does his analysis square with Justice Alito's description of the modern doctrines of substantive due process and equal protection?)
- Does this case represent either a rejection of or an alternative to the Court's approach to substantive due process in *Glucksburg*?
- Is this a "substantive due process" or "equal protection" decision, or both? How do the two theories relate to each other here?
- Justice Scalia asks, "Even after the opinion has formally disclaimed reliance upon principles of federalism, mentions of 'the usual tradition of recognizing and accepting state definitions of marriage' continue. What to make of this?" What do you make of it? Has "federalism" now become relevant to a due process inquiry and, if so, how?
- Could Justice Kennedy's approach be adapted to protect the "right to use marijuana for medical purposes" that the Ninth Circuit denied in *Raich*?
- Does the majority provide arguments to support constitutional challenges to *state* laws restricting marriage to opposite sex couples? If so, what do you make of the majority's emphasis on federalism? Do you think that the "community's considered perspective" on the scope of marriage will be allowed by the Court to cut both ways?

## UNITED STATES v. WINDSOR

*No. 12-307. | Decided June 26, 2013*

JUSTICE KENNEDY delivered the opinion of the Court. . . .

### I

In 1996, as some States were beginning to consider the concept of same-sex marriage, and before any State had acted to permit it, Congress enacted the Defense of Marriage Act (DOMA). DOMA contains two operative sections: Section 2, which has not been challenged here, allows States to refuse to recognize same-sex marriages performed under the laws of other States. Section 3 is at issue here. It amends the Dictionary Act in Title 1, §7, of the United States Code to provide a federal definition of "marriage" and "spouse." Section 3 of DOMA provides as follows:

> In determining the meaning of any Act of Congress, or of any ruling, regulation, or interpretation of the various administrative bureaus and agencies of the United States, the word "marriage" means only a legal union between one man and one woman as husband and wife, and the word "spouse" refers only to a person of the opposite sex who is a husband or a wife.

The definitional provision does not by its terms forbid States from enacting laws permitting same-sex marriages or civil unions or providing state benefits to residents in that status. The enactment's comprehensive definition of marriage for purposes of all federal statutes and other regulations or directives covered by its terms, however, does control over 1,000 federal laws in which marital or spousal status is addressed as a matter of federal law.

Edith Windsor and Thea Spyer met in New York City in 1963 and began a long-term relationship. Windsor and Spyer registered as domestic partners when New York City gave that right to same-sex couples in 1993. Concerned about Spyer's health, the couple made the 2007 trip to Canada for their marriage, but they continued to reside in New York City. The State of New York deems their Ontario marriage to be a valid one.

Spyer died in February 2009, and left her entire estate to Windsor. Because DOMA denies federal recognition to same-sex spouses, Windsor did not qualify for the marital exemption from the federal estate tax, which excludes from taxation "any interest in property which passes or has passed from the decedent to his surviving spouse." Windsor paid $363,053 in estate taxes and sought a refund. The Internal Revenue Service denied the refund, concluding that, under DOMA, Windsor was not a "surviving spouse." Windsor commenced this refund suit in the United States District Court for the Southern District of New York. She contended that DOMA violates the guarantee of equal protection, as applied to the Federal Government through the Fifth Amendment. . . .

III

When at first Windsor and Spyer longed to marry, neither New York nor any other State granted them that right. After waiting some years, in 2007 they traveled to Ontario to be married there. It seems fair to conclude that, until recent years, many citizens had not even considered the possibility that two persons of the same sex might aspire to occupy the same status and dignity as that of a man and woman in lawful marriage. For marriage between a man and a woman no doubt had been thought of by most people as essential to the very definition of that term and to its role and function throughout the history of civilization. That belief, for many who long have held it, became even more urgent, more cherished when challenged. For others, however, came the beginnings of a new perspective, a new insight. Accordingly some States concluded that same-sex marriage ought to be given recognition and validity in the law for those same-sex couples who wish to define themselves by their commitment to each other. The limitation of lawful marriage to heterosexual couples, which for centuries had been deemed both necessary and fundamental, came to be seen in New York and certain other States as an unjust exclusion. Slowly at first and then in rapid course, the laws of New York came to acknowledge the urgency of this issue for same-sex couples who wanted to affirm their commitment to one another before their children, their family, their friends, and their community. And so New York recognized same-sex marriages performed elsewhere; and then it later amended its own marriage laws to permit same-sex marriage. New York, in common with, as of this writing, 11 other States and the District of Columbia, decided that same-sex couples should have the right to marry and so live with pride in themselves and their union and in a status of equality with all other married persons. After a statewide deliberative process that enabled its citizens to discuss and weigh arguments for and against same-sex marriage, New York acted to enlarge the definition of marriage to correct what its citizens and elected representatives perceived to be an injustice that they had not earlier known or understood.

Against this background of lawful same-sex marriage in some States, the design, purpose, and effect of DOMA should be considered as the beginning point in deciding whether it is valid under the Constitution. By history and tradition the definition and regulation of marriage, as will be discussed in more detail, has been treated as being within the authority and realm of the separate States. Yet it is further established that Congress, in enacting discrete statutes, can make determinations that bear on marital rights and privileges. . . . [W]hen the Federal Government acts in the exercise of its own proper authority, it has a wide choice of the mechanisms and means to adopt. See *McCulloch v. Maryland* (1819). Congress has the power both to ensure efficiency in the administration of its programs and to choose what larger goals and policies to pursue. Other precedents involving congressional statutes which affect marriages and family status further illustrate this point. In addressing the interaction of state domestic relations and federal immigration law Congress determined that marriages "entered into for the purpose of procuring an alien's admission [to the United States] as an immigrant" will not qualify the noncitizen for that status, even if the noncitizen's marriage is valid and proper for state-law purposes. And in establishing income-based criteria for Social Security benefits, Congress decided that although state law would determine in general who qualifies as an applicant's spouse, common-law marriages also should be recognized, regardless of any particular State's view on these relationships.

Though these discrete examples establish the constitutionality of limited federal laws that regulate the meaning of marriage in order to further federal policy, DOMA has a far greater reach; for it enacts a directive applicable to over 1,000 federal statutes and the whole realm of federal regulations. And its operation is directed to a class of persons that the laws of New York, and of 11 other States, have sought to protect.

In order to assess the validity of that intervention it is necessary to discuss the extent of the state power and authority over marriage as a matter of history and tradition. State laws defining and regulating marriage, of course, must respect the constitutional rights of persons, see, *e.g., Loving v. Virginia* (1967); but, subject to those guarantees, "regulation of domestic relations" is "an area that has long been regarded as a virtually exclusive province of the States." *Sosna v. Iowa* (1975).

The recognition of civil marriages is central to state domestic relations law applicable to its residents and citizens. See *Williams v. North Carolina* (1942) ("Each state as a sovereign has a rightful and legitimate concern in the marital status of persons domiciled within its borders"). The definition of marriage is the foundation of the State's broader authority to regulate the subject of domestic relations with respect to the "[p]rotection of offspring, property interests, and the enforcement of marital responsibilities." *Ibid.* "[T]he states, at the time of the adoption of the Constitution, possessed full power over the subject of marriage and divorce . . . [and] the Constitution delegated no authority to the Government of the United States on the subject of marriage and divorce." *Haddock v. Haddock* (1906); see also *In re Burrus* (1890) ("The whole subject of the domestic relations of husband and wife, parent and child, belongs to the laws of the States and not to the laws of the United States").

Consistent with this allocation of authority, the Federal Government, through our history, has deferred to state-law policy decisions with respect to domestic relations. In *De Sylva v. Ballentine* (1956), for example, the Court held that, "[t]o decide who is the widow or widower of a deceased author, or who are his executors or next of kin," under the Copyright Act "requires a reference to the law of the State which created those legal relationships" because "there is no federal law of domestic relations." In order to respect this principle, the federal courts, as a general rule, do not adjudicate issues of marital status even when there might otherwise be a basis for federal jurisdiction. See *Ankenbrandt v. Richards* (1992). Federal courts will not hear divorce and custody cases even if they arise in diversity because of "the virtually exclusive primacy . . . of the States in the regulation of domestic relations." *Id.* (Blackmun, J., concurring in judgment).

The significance of state responsibilities for the definition and regulation of marriage dates to the Nation's beginning; for "when the Constitution was adopted the common understanding was that the domestic relations of husband

and wife and parent and child were matters reserved to the States." *Ohio ex rel. Popovici v. Agler* (1930). Marriage laws vary in some respects from State to State. For example, the required minimum age is 16 in Vermont, but only 13 in New Hampshire. Likewise the permissible degree of consanguinity can vary (most States permit first cousins to marry, but a handful—such as Iowa and Washington—prohibit the practice). But these rules are in every event consistent within each State.

Against this background DOMA rejects the long-established precept that the incidents, benefits, and obligations of marriage are uniform for all married couples within each State, though they may vary, subject to constitutional guarantees, from one State to the next. Despite these considerations, it is unnecessary to decide whether this federal intrusion on state power is a violation of the Constitution because it disrupts the federal balance. The State's power in defining the marital relation is of central relevance in this case quite apart from principles of federalism. Here the State's decision to give this class of persons the right to marry conferred upon them a dignity and status of immense import. When the State used its historic and essential authority to define the marital relation in this way, its role and its power in making the decision enhanced the recognition, dignity, and protection of the class in their own community. DOMA, because of its reach and extent, departs from this history and tradition of reliance on state law to define marriage. " '[D]iscriminations of an unusual character especially suggest careful consideration to determine whether they are obnoxious to the constitutional provision.' " *Romer v. Evans* (1996) (quoting *Louisville Gas & Elec. Co. v. Coleman* (1928)).

The Federal Government uses this state-defined class for the opposite purpose—to impose restrictions and disabilities. That result requires this Court now to address whether the resulting injury and indignity is a deprivation of an essential part of the liberty protected by the Fifth Amendment. What the State of New York treats as alike the federal law deems unlike by a law designed to injure the same class the State seeks to protect.

In acting first to recognize and then to allow same-sex marriages, New York was responding "to the initiative of those who [sought] a voice in shaping the destiny of their own times." *Bond v. United States* (2011). These actions were without doubt a proper exercise of its sovereign authority within our federal system, all in the way that the Framers of the Constitution intended. The dynamics of state government in the federal system are to allow the formation of consensus respecting the way the members of a discrete community treat each other in their daily contact and constant interaction with each other.

The States' interest in defining and regulating the marital relation, subject to constitutional guarantees, stems from the understanding that marriage is more than a routine classification for purposes of certain statutory benefits. Private, consensual sexual intimacy between two adult persons of the same sex may not be punished by the State, and it can form "but one element in a personal bond that is more enduring." *Lawrence v. Texas* (2003). By its recognition of the validity of same-sex marriages performed in other jurisdictions and then by authorizing same-sex unions and same-sex marriages, New York sought to give further protection and dignity to that bond. For same-sex couples who wished to be married, the State acted to give their lawful conduct a lawful status. This status is a far-reaching legal acknowledgment of the intimate relationship between two people, a relationship deemed by the State worthy of dignity in the community equal with all other marriages. It reflects both the community's considered perspective on the historical roots of the institution of marriage and its evolving understanding of the meaning of equality.

IV

DOMA seeks to injure the very class New York seeks to protect. By doing so it violates basic due process and equal protection principles applicable to the Federal Government. See U.S. Const., Amdt. 5; *Bolling v. Sharpe* (1954). The Constitution's guarantee of equality "must at the very least mean that a bare congressional desire to harm a politically unpopular group cannot" justify disparate treatment of that group. *Department of Agriculture v. Moreno* (1973). In determining whether a law is motived by an improper animus or purpose, "[d]iscriminations of an unusual character" especially require careful consideration. *Romer*. DOMA cannot survive under these principles. The responsibility of the States for the regulation of domestic relations is an important indicator of the substantial societal impact the State's classifications have in the daily lives and customs of its people. DOMA's unusual deviation from the usual tradition of recognizing and accepting state definitions of marriage here operates to deprive same-sex couples of the benefits and responsibilities that come with the federal recognition of their marriages. This is strong evidence of a law having the purpose and effect of disapproval of that class. The avowed purpose and practical effect of the law here in question are to impose a disadvantage, a separate status, and so a stigma upon all who enter into same-sex marriages made lawful by the unquestioned authority of the States. The history of DOMA's enactment and its own text demonstrate that interference with the equal dignity of same-sex marriages, a dignity conferred by the States in the exercise of their sovereign power, was more than an incidental effect of the federal statute. It was its essence. The House Report announced its conclusion that "it is both appropriate and necessary for Congress to do what it can to defend the institution of traditional heterosexual marriage. . . . H.R. 3396 is appropriately entitled the 'Defense of Marriage Act.' The effort to redefine 'marriage' to extend to homosexual couples is a truly radical proposal that would fundamentally alter the institution of marriage." H.R. Rep. No. 104-664 (1996). The House concluded that DOMA expresses "both moral disapproval of homosexuality, and a moral conviction that heterosexuality better comports with traditional (especially Judeo–Christian) morality." The stated purpose of the law was to promote an "interest in protecting the traditional moral teachings reflected in heterosexual-only marriage laws." Were there any doubt of this far-reaching purpose, the title of the Act confirms it: The Defense of Marriage.

The arguments put forward by [the Bipartisan Legal Advisory Group (BLAG) of the House of Representatives] are just as candid about the congressional purpose to influence or interfere with state sovereign choices about who may be married. As the title and dynamics of the bill indicate, its purpose is to discourage enactment of state same-sex marriage laws and to restrict the freedom and choice of couples married under those laws if they are enacted. The congressional goal was "to put a thumb on the scales and influence a state's decision as to how to shape its own marriage laws." [*Massachusetts v. United States Dept. of Health and Human Servs.* (C.A.1 2012)]. The Act's demonstrated purpose is to ensure that if any State decides to recognize same-sex marriages, those unions will be treated as second-class marriages for purposes of federal law. This raises a most serious question under the Constitution's Fifth Amendment.

DOMA's operation in practice confirms this purpose. When New York adopted a law to permit same-sex marriage, it sought to eliminate inequality; but DOMA frustrates that objective through a system-wide enactment with no identified connection to any particular area of federal law. DOMA writes inequality into the entire United States Code. The particular case at hand concerns the estate tax, but DOMA is more than a simple determination of what should or should not be allowed as an estate tax refund. Among the over 1,000 statutes and numerous federal regulations that DOMA controls are laws pertaining to Social Security, housing, taxes, criminal sanctions, copyright, and veterans' benefits.

DOMA's principal effect is to identify a subset of state-sanctioned marriages and make them unequal. The principal purpose is to impose inequality, not for other reasons like governmental efficiency. Responsibilities, as well as rights, enhance the dignity and integrity of the person. And DOMA contrives to deprive some couples married under the laws of their State, but not other couples, of both rights and responsibilities. By creating two contradictory marriage regimes within the same State, DOMA forces same-sex couples to live as married for the purpose of state law but unmarried for the purpose of federal law, thus diminishing the stability and predictability of basic personal relations the State has found it proper to acknowledge and protect. By this dynamic DOMA undermines both the public and private significance of state-sanctioned same-sex marriages; for it tells those couples, and all the world, that their otherwise valid marriages are unworthy of federal recognition. This places same-sex couples in an unstable position of being in a second-tier marriage. The differentiation demeans the couple, whose moral and sexual choices the Constitution protects, see *Lawrence,* and whose relationship the State has sought to dignify. And it humiliates tens of thousands of children now being raised by same-sex couples. The law in question makes it even more difficult for the children to understand the integrity and closeness of their own family and its concord with other families in their community and in their daily lives.

Under DOMA, same-sex married couples have their lives burdened, by reason of government decree, in visible and public ways. By its great reach, DOMA touches many aspects of married and family life, from the mundane to the profound. It prevents same-sex married couples from obtaining government healthcare benefits they would otherwise receive. It deprives them of the Bankruptcy Code's special protections for domestic-support obligations. It forces them to follow a complicated procedure to file their state and federal taxes jointly.

Brief for Federalism Scholars as *Amici Curiae*. It prohibits them from being buried together in veterans' cemeteries. For certain married couples, DOMA's unequal effects are even more serious. The federal penal code makes it a crime to "assaul[t], kidna[p], or murde[r] . . . a member of the immediate family" of "a United States official, a United States judge, [or] a Federal law enforcement officer," with the intent to influence or retaliate against that official. Although a "spouse" qualifies as a member of the officer's "immediate family," DOMA makes this protection inapplicable to same-sex spouses.

DOMA also brings financial harm to children of same-sex couples. It raises the cost of health care for families by taxing health benefits provided by employers to their workers' same-sex spouses. And it denies or reduces benefits allowed to families upon the loss of a spouse and parent, benefits that are an integral part of family security.

DOMA divests married same-sex couples of the duties and responsibilities that are an essential part of married life and that they in most cases would be honored to accept were DOMA not in force. For instance, because it is expected that spouses will support each other as they pursue educational opportunities, federal law takes into consideration a spouse's income in calculating a student's federal financial aid eligibility. Same-sex married couples are exempt from this requirement. The same is true with respect to federal ethics rules. Federal executive and agency officials are prohibited from "participat[ing] personally and substantially" in matters as to which they or their spouses have a financial interest. A similar statute prohibits Senators, Senate employees, and their spouses from accepting high-value gifts from certain sources, and another mandates detailed financial disclosures by numerous high-ranking officials and their spouses. Under DOMA, however, these Government-integrity rules do not apply to same-sex spouses.

* * *

The power the Constitution grants it also restrains. And though Congress has great authority to design laws to fit its own conception of sound national policy, it cannot deny the liberty protected by the Due Process Clause of the Fifth Amendment. What has been explained to this point should more than suffice to establish that the principal purpose and the necessary effect of this law are to demean those persons who are in a lawful same-sex marriage. This requires the Court to hold, as it now does, that DOMA is unconstitutional as a deprivation of the liberty of the person protected by the Fifth Amendment of the Constitution.

The liberty protected by the Fifth Amendment's Due Process Clause contains within it the prohibition against denying to any person the equal protection of the laws. See *Bolling*; *Adarand Constructors, Inc. v. Peña* (1995). While the Fifth Amendment itself withdraws from Government the power to degrade or demean in the way this law does, the equal protection guarantee of the Fourteenth Amendment makes that Fifth Amendment right all the more specific and all the better understood and preserved.

The class to which DOMA directs its restrictions and restraints are those persons who are joined in same-sex marriages made lawful by the State. DOMA singles out a class of persons deemed by a State entitled to recognition and protection to enhance their own liberty. It imposes a disability on the class by refusing to acknowledge a status the State finds to be dignified and proper. DOMA instructs all federal officials, and indeed all persons with whom same-sex couples interact, including their own children, that their marriage is less worthy than the marriages of others. The federal statute is invalid, for no legitimate purpose overcomes the purpose and effect to disparage and to injure those whom the State, by its marriage laws, sought to protect in personhood and dignity. By seeking to displace this protection and treating those persons as living in marriages less respected than others, the federal statute is in violation of the Fifth Amendment. This opinion and its holding are confined to those lawful marriages.

The judgment of the Court of Appeals for the Second Circuit is affirmed.

*It is so ordered.*

CHIEF JUSTICE ROBERTS, dissenting. . . .

[W]hile I disagree with the result to which the majority's analysis leads it in this case, I think it more important to point out that its analysis leads no further. The Court does not have before it, and the logic of its opinion does not decide, the distinct question whether the States, in the exercise of their "historic and essential authority to define the marital relation," may continue to utilize the traditional definition of marriage.

The majority goes out of its way to make this explicit in the penultimate sentence of its opinion. It states that "[t]his opinion and its holding are confined to those lawful marriages,"—referring to same-sex marriages that a State has already recognized as a result of the local "community's considered perspective on the historical roots of the institution of marriage and its evolving understanding of the meaning of equality." Justice Scalia believes this is a "bald, unreasoned disclaime[r]." In my view, though, the disclaimer is a logical and necessary consequence of the argument the majority has chosen to adopt. The dominant theme of the majority opinion is that the Federal Government's intrusion into an area "central to state domestic relations law applicable to its residents and citizens" is sufficiently "unusual" to set off alarm bells. I think the majority goes off course, as I have said, but it is undeniable that its judgment is based on federalism.

The majority extensively chronicles DOMA's departure from the normal allocation of responsibility between State and Federal Governments, emphasizing that DOMA "rejects the long-established precept that the incidents, benefits, and obligations of marriage are uniform for all married couples within each State." But there is no such departure when one State adopts or keeps a definition of marriage that differs from that of its neighbor, for it is entirely expected that state definitions would "vary, subject to constitutional guarantees, from one State to the next." Thus, while "[t]he State's power in defining the marital relation is of central relevance" to the majority's decision to strike down DOMA here, that power will come into play on the other side of the board in future cases about the constitutionality of state marriage definitions. So too will the concerns for state diversity and sovereignty that weigh against DOMA's constitutionality in this case. It is not just this central feature of the majority's analysis that is unique to DOMA, but many considerations on the periphery as well. For example, the majority focuses on the legislative history and title of this particular Act; those statute-specific considerations will, of course, be irrelevant in future cases about different statutes. The majority emphasizes that DOMA was a "systemwide enactment with no identified connection to any particular area of federal law," but a State's definition of marriage "is the foundation of the State's broader authority to regulate the subject of domestic relations with respect to the '[p]rotection of offspring, property interests, and the enforcement of marital responsibilities.'" And the federal decision undermined (in the majority's view) the "dignity [already] conferred by the States in the exercise of their sovereign power," whereas a State's decision whether to expand the definition of marriage from its traditional contours involves no similar concern.

We may in the future have to resolve challenges to state marriage definitions affecting same-sex couples. That issue, however, is not before us in this case. . . . I write only to highlight the limits of the majority's holding and reasoning today, lest its opinion be taken to resolve not only a question that I believe is not properly before us—DOMA's constitutionality—but also a question that all agree, and the Court explicitly acknowledges, is not at issue.

JUSTICE SCALIA, with whom JUSTICE THOMAS joins. . . .

This case is about power in several respects. It is about the power of our people to govern themselves, and the power of this Court to pronounce the law. Today's opinion aggrandizes the latter, with the predictable consequence of diminishing the former. . . .

II

[Because of the absence of standing,] I think that this Court has, and the Court of Appeals had, no power to decide this suit. We should vacate the decision below and remand to the Court of Appeals for the Second Circuit, with instructions to dismiss the appeal. Given that the majority has volunteered its view of the merits, however, I proceed to discuss that as well.

A

There are many remarkable things about the majority's merits holding. The first is how rootless and shifting its justifications are. For example, the opinion starts with seven full pages about the traditional power of States to define domestic relations—initially fooling many readers, I am sure, into thinking that this is a federalism opinion. But we are eventually told that "it is unnecessary to decide whether this federal intrusion on state power is a violation of the Constitution," and that "[t]he State's power in defining the marital relation is of central relevance in this case quite apart from principles of federalism" because "the State's decision to give this class of persons the right to marry conferred upon them a dignity and status of immense import." But no one questions the power of the States to define marriage (with the concomitant conferral of dignity and status), so what is the point of devoting seven pages to describing how long and well established that power is? Even after the opinion has formally disclaimed reliance upon principles of federalism, mentions of "the usual tradition of recognizing and accepting state definitions of marriage" continue. What to make of this? The opinion never explains. My guess is that the majority, while reluctant to suggest that defining the meaning of "marriage" in federal statutes is unsupported by any of the Federal Government's enumerated powers,[1] nonetheless needs some rhetorical basis to support its pretense that today's prohibition of laws excluding same-sex marriage is confined to the Federal Government (leaving the second, state-law shoe to be dropped later, maybe next Term). But I am only guessing.

Equally perplexing are the opinion's references to "the Constitution's guarantee of equality." Near the end of the opinion, we are told that although the "equal protection guarantee of the Fourteenth Amendment makes [the] Fifth Amendment [due process] right all the more specific and all the better understood and preserved"—what can *that* mean?—"the Fifth Amendment itself withdraws from Government the power to degrade or demean in the way this law does." The only possible interpretation of this statement is that the Equal Protection Clause, even the Equal Protection Clause as incorporated in the Due Process Clause, is not the basis for today's holding. But the portion of the majority opinion that explains why DOMA is unconstitutional (Part IV) begins by citing *Bolling v. Sharpe* (1954), *Department of Agriculture v. Moreno* (1973), and *Romer v. Evans* (1996)—*all* of which are equal-protection cases.[2] And those three cases are the *only* authorities that the Court cites in Part IV about the Constitution's meaning, except for its citation of *Lawrence v. Texas* (2003) (not an equal-protection case) to support its passing assertion that the Constitution protects the "moral and sexual choices" of same-sex couples.

Moreover, if this is meant to be an equal-protection opinion, it is a confusing one. The opinion does not resolve and indeed does not even mention what had been the central question in this litigation: whether, under the Equal Protection Clause, laws restricting marriage to a man and a woman are reviewed for more than mere rationality. That is the issue that divided the parties and the court below. In accord with my previously expressed skepticism about the Court's "tiers of scrutiny" approach, I would review this classification only for its rationality. See *United States v. Virginia* (1996) (Scalia, J., dissenting). As nearly as I can tell, the Court agrees with that; its opinion does not apply strict scrutiny, and

1. Such a suggestion would be impossible, given the Federal Government's long history of making pronouncements regarding marriage—for example, conditioning Utah's entry into the Union upon its prohibition of polygamy. See Act of July 16, 1894 ("The constitution [of Utah]" must provide "perfect toleration of religious sentiment," "*Provided,* That polygamous or plural marriages are forever prohibited").

2. Since the Equal Protection Clause technically applies only against the States, *Bolling* and *Moreno*, dealing with federal action, relied upon "the equal protection component of the Due Process Clause of the Fifth Amendment," *Moreno*.

its central propositions are taken from rational-basis cases like *Moreno*. But the Court certainly does not *apply* anything that resembles that deferential framework. See *Heller v. Doe* (1993) (a classification "must be upheld . . . if there is any reasonably conceivable state of facts" that could justify it).

The majority opinion need not get into the strict-vs.-rational-basis scrutiny question, and need not justify its holding under either, because it says that DOMA is unconstitutional as "a deprivation of the liberty of the person protected by the Fifth Amendment of the Constitution"; that it violates "basic due process" principles; and that it inflicts an "injury and indignity" of a kind that denies "an essential part of the liberty protected by the Fifth Amendment." The majority never utters the dread words "substantive due process," perhaps sensing the disrepute into which that doctrine has fallen, but that is what those statements mean. Yet the opinion does not argue that same-sex marriage is "deeply rooted in this Nation's history and tradition," *Washington v. Glucksberg* (1997), a claim that would of course be quite absurd. So would the further suggestion (also necessary, under our substantive-due-process precedents) that a world in which DOMA exists is one bereft of "ordered liberty." *Id.* (quoting *Palko v. Connecticut* (1937)).

Some might conclude that this loaf could have used a while longer in the oven. But that would be wrong; it is already overcooked. The most expert care in preparation cannot redeem a bad recipe. The sum of all the Court's nonspecific hand-waving is that this law is invalid (maybe on equal-protection grounds, maybe on substantive-due-process grounds, and perhaps with some amorphous federalism component playing a role) because it is motivated by a "bare . . . desire to harm" couples in same-sex marriages. It is this proposition with which I will therefore engage.

### B

As I have observed before, the Constitution does not forbid the government to enforce traditional moral and sexual norms. See *Lawrence v. Texas* (2003) (Scalia, J., dissenting). I will not swell the U.S. Reports with restatements of that point. It is enough to say that the Constitution neither requires nor forbids our society to approve of same-sex marriage, much as it neither requires nor forbids us to approve of no-fault divorce, polygamy, or the consumption of alcohol. However, even setting aside traditional moral disapproval of same-sex marriage (or indeed same-sex sex), there are many perfectly valid—indeed, downright boring—justifying rationales for this legislation. Their existence ought to be the end of this case. For they give the lie to the Court's conclusion that only those with hateful hearts could have voted "aye" on this Act. And more importantly, they serve to make the contents of the legislators' hearts quite irrelevant: "It is a familiar principle of constitutional law that this Court will not strike down an otherwise constitutional statute on the basis of an alleged illicit legislative motive." *United States v. O'Brien* (1968). Or at least it *was* a familiar principle. By holding to the contrary, the majority has declared open season on any law that (in the opinion of the law's opponents and any panel of like-minded federal judges) can be characterized as mean-spirited.

The majority concludes that the only motive for this Act was the "bare . . . desire to harm a politically unpopular group." Bear in mind that the object of this condemnation is not the legislature of some once-Confederate Southern state (familiar objects of the Court's scorn), but our respected coordinate branches, the Congress and Presidency of the United States. Laying such a charge against them should require the most extraordinary evidence, and I would have thought that every attempt would be made to indulge a more anodyne explanation for the statute. The majority does the opposite—affirmatively concealing from the reader the arguments that exist in justification. It makes only a passing mention of the "arguments put forward" by the Act's defenders, and does not even trouble to paraphrase or describe them. I imagine that this is because it is harder to maintain the illusion of the Act's supporters as unhinged members of a wild-eyed lynch mob when one first describes their views as *they* see them.

To choose just one of these defenders' arguments, DOMA avoids difficult choice-of-law issues that will now arise absent a uniform federal definition of marriage. See, *e.g.*, Baude, Beyond DOMA: Choice of State Law in Federal Statutes, 64 Stan. L. Rev. 1371 (2012). Imagine a pair of women who marry in Albany and then move to Alabama, which does not "recognize as valid any marriage of parties of the same sex." When the couple files their next federal tax return, may it be a joint one? Which State's law controls, for federal-law purposes: their State of celebration (which recognizes the marriage) or their State of domicile (which does not)? (Does the answer depend on whether they were just visiting in Albany?) Are these questions to be answered as a matter of federal common law, or perhaps by borrowing a State's choice-of-law rules? If so, *which* State's? And what about States where the status of an out-of-state same-sex marriage is an unsettled question under local law? DOMA avoided all of this uncertainty by specifying which marriages would be recognized for federal purposes. That is a classic purpose for a definitional provision.

Further, DOMA preserves the intended effects of prior legislation against then-unforeseen changes in circumstance. When Congress provided (for example) that a special estate-tax exemption would exist for spouses, this exemption reached only *opposite-sex* spouses—those being the only sort that were recognized in *any* State at the time of DOMA's passage. When it became clear that changes in state law might one day alter that balance, DOMA's definitional section was enacted to ensure that state-level experimentation did not automatically alter the basic operation of federal law, unless and until Congress made the further judgment to do so on its own. That is not animus—just stabilizing prudence. Congress has hardly demonstrated itself unwilling to make such further, revising judgments upon due deliberation. See, *e.g.*, Don't Ask, Don't Tell Repeal Act of 2010.

The Court mentions none of this. Instead, it accuses the Congress that enacted this law and the President who signed it of something much worse than, for example, having acted in excess of enumerated federal powers—or even having drawn distinctions that prove to be irrational. Those legal errors may be made in good faith, errors though they are. But the majority says that the supporters of this Act acted with *malice*—with *the "purpose"* "to disparage and to injure" same-sex couples. It says that the motivation for DOMA was to "demean," to "impose inequality," to "impose . . . a stigma," to deny people "equal dignity," to brand gay people as "unworthy," and to "*humiliat*[*e*]" their children (emphasis added).

I am sure these accusations are quite untrue. To be sure (as the majority points out), the legislation is called the Defense of Marriage Act. But to defend traditional marriage is not to condemn, demean, or humiliate those who would prefer other arrangements, any more than to defend the Constitution of the United States is to condemn, demean, or humiliate other constitutions. To hurl such accusations so casually demeans *this institution*. In the majority's judgment, any resistance to its holding is beyond the pale of reasoned disagreement. To question its high-handed invalidation of a presumptively valid statute is to act (the majority is sure) with *the purpose* to "disparage," "injure," "degrade," "demean," and "humiliate" our fellow human beings, our fellow citizens, who are homosexual. All that, simply for supporting an Act that did no more than codify an aspect of marriage that had been unquestioned in our society for most of its existence—indeed, had been unquestioned in virtually all societies for virtually all of human history. It is one thing for a society to elect change; it is another for a court of law to impose change by adjudging those who oppose it *hostes humani generis,* enemies of the human race.

* * *

The penultimate sentence of the majority's opinion is a naked declaration that "[t]his opinion and its holding are confined" to those couples "joined in same-sex marriages made lawful by the State." I have heard such "bald, unreasoned disclaimer[s]" before. *Lawrence*. When the Court declared a constitutional right to homosexual sodomy, we were assured that the case had nothing, nothing at all to do with "whether the government must give formal recognition to any relationship that homosexual persons seek to enter." Now we are told that DOMA is invalid because it "demeans the couple, whose moral and sexual choices the Constitution protects,"—with an accompanying citation of *Lawrence*. It takes real cheek for today's majority to assure us, as it is going out the door, that a constitutional requirement to give formal recognition to same-sex marriage is not at issue here—when what has preceded that assurance is a lecture on how superior the majority's moral judgment in favor of same-sex marriage is to the Congress's hateful moral judgment against it. I promise you this: The only thing that will "confine" the Court's holding is its sense of what it can get away with. I do not mean to suggest disagreement with The Chief Justice's view that lower federal courts and state courts can distinguish today's case when the issue before them is state denial of marital status to same-sex couples—or even that this Court could *theoretically* do so. Lord, an opinion with such scatter-shot rationales as this one (federalism noises among them) can be distinguished in many ways. And deserves to be. State and lower federal courts should take the Court at its word and distinguish away.

In my opinion, however, the view that *this* Court will take of state prohibition of same-sex marriage is indicated beyond mistaking by today's opinion. As I have said, the real rationale of today's opinion, whatever disappearing trail of its legalistic argle-bargle one chooses to follow, is that DOMA is motivated by "bare . . . desire to harm" couples in same-sex marriages. How easy it is, indeed how inevitable, to reach the same conclusion with regard to state laws denying same-sex couples marital status. Consider how easy (inevitable) it is to make the following substitutions in a passage from today's opinion:

> *This state law's* principal effect is to identify a subset of *constitutionally protected sexual relationships*, see *Lawrence,* and make them unequal. The principal purpose is to impose inequality, not for other reasons like governmental efficiency. Responsibilities, as well as rights, enhance the dignity and integrity of the person. And *this state law* contrives to deprive some couples *enjoying constitutionally protected sexual relationships,* but not other couples, of both rights and responsibilities.

Or try this passage:

> *This state law* tells those couples, and all the world, that their otherwise valid *relationships* are unworthy of *state* recognition. This places same-sex couples in an unstable position of being in a second-tier *relationship*. The differentiation demeans the couple, whose moral and sexual choices the Constitution protects, see *Lawrence*. . . .

Or this, which does not even require alteration, except as to the invented number:

> And it humiliates thousands of children now being raised by same-sex couples. The law in question makes it even more difficult for the children to understand the integrity and closeness of their own family and its concord with other families in their community and in their daily lives.

Similarly transposable passages—deliberately transposable, I think—abound. In sum, that Court which finds it so horrific that Congress irrationally and hatefully robbed same-sex couples of the "personhood and dignity" which state legislatures conferred upon them, will of a certitude be similarly appalled by state legislatures' irrational and hateful failure to acknowledge that "personhood and dignity" in the first place. As far as this Court is concerned, no one should be fooled; it is just a matter of listening and waiting for the other shoe.

By formally declaring anyone opposed to same-sex marriage an enemy of human decency, the majority arms well every challenger to a state law restricting marriage to its traditional definition. Henceforth those challengers will lead with this Court's declaration that there is "no legitimate purpose" served by such a law, and will claim that the traditional definition has "the purpose and effect to disparage and to injure" the "personhood and dignity" of same-sex couples. The majority's limiting assurance will be meaningless in the face of language like that, as the majority well knows. That is why the language is there. The result will be a judicial distortion of our society's debate over marriage—a debate that can seem in need of our clumsy "help" only to a member of this institution.

As to that debate: Few public controversies touch an institution so central to the lives of so many, and few inspire such attendant passion by good people on all sides. Few public controversies will ever demonstrate so vividly the beauty of what our Framers gave us, a gift the Court pawns today to buy its stolen moment in the spotlight: a system of government that permits us to rule *ourselves*. Since DOMA's passage, citizens on all sides of the question have seen victories and they have seen defeats. There have been plebiscites, legislation, persuasion, and loud voices—in other words, democracy. Victories in one place for some, see North Carolina Const., Amdt. 1 (providing that "[m]arriage between one man and one woman is the only domestic legal union that shall be valid or recognized in this State") (approved by a popular vote, 61% to 39% on May 8, 2012), are offset by victories in other places for others, see Maryland Question 6 (establishing "that Maryland's civil marriage laws allow gay and lesbian couples to obtain a civil marriage license") (approved by a popular vote, 52% to 48%, on November 6, 2012). Even in a *single State,* the question has come out differently on different occasions. Compare Maine Question 1 (permitting "the State of Maine to issue marriage licenses to same-sex couples") (approved by a popular vote, 53% to 47%, on November 6, 2012) with Maine Question 1 (rejecting "the new law that lets same-sex couples marry") (approved by a popular vote, 53% to 47%, on November 3, 2009).

In the majority's telling, this story is black-and-white: Hate your neighbor or come along with us. The truth is more complicated. It is hard to admit that one's political opponents are not monsters, especially in a struggle like this one, and the challenge in the end proves more than today's Court can handle. Too bad. A reminder that disagreement over something so fundamental as marriage can still be politically legitimate would have been a fit task for what in earlier times was called the judicial temperament. We might have covered ourselves with honor today, by promising all sides of this debate that it was theirs to settle and that we would respect their resolution. We might have let the People decide.

But that the majority will not do. Some will rejoice in today's decision, and some will despair at it; that is the nature of a controversy that matters so much to so many. But the Court has cheated both sides, robbing the winners of an honest victory, and the losers of the peace that comes from a fair defeat. We owed both of them better. I dissent.

JUSTICE ALITO, with whom JUSTICE THOMAS joins as to Parts II and III, dissenting.

Our Nation is engaged in a heated debate about same-sex marriage. That debate is, at bottom, about the nature of the institution of marriage. Respondent Edith Windsor, supported by the United States, asks this Court to intervene in that debate, and although she couches her argument in different terms, what she seeks is a holding that enshrines in the Constitution a particular understanding of marriage under which the sex of the partners makes no difference. The Constitution, however, does not dictate that choice. It leaves the choice to the people, acting through their elected representatives at both the federal and state levels. I would therefore hold that Congress did not violate Windsor's constitutional rights by enacting §3 of the Defense of Marriage Act (DOMA), which defines the meaning of marriage under federal statutes that either confer upon married persons certain federal benefits or impose upon them certain federal obligations. . . .

II

. . . Same-sex marriage presents a highly emotional and important question of public policy—but not a difficult question of constitutional law. The Constitution does not guarantee the right to enter into a same-sex marriage. Indeed, no provision of the Constitution speaks to the issue.

The Court has sometimes found the Due Process Clauses to have a substantive component that guarantees liberties beyond the absence of physical restraint. And the Court's holding that "DOMA is unconstitutional as a deprivation of the liberty of the person protected by the Fifth Amendment of the Constitution," suggests that substantive due process may partially underlie the Court's decision today. But it is well established that any "substantive" component to the Due Process Clause protects only "those fundamental rights and liberties which are, objectively, 'deeply rooted in this Nation's history and tradition,'" *Washington v. Glucksberg* (1997), as well as "'implicit in the concept of ordered liberty,' such that 'neither liberty nor justice would exist if they were sacrificed.'" *Glucksberg* (quoting *Palko v. Connecticut* (1937)).

It is beyond dispute that the right to same-sex marriage is not deeply rooted in this Nation's history and tradition. In this country, no State permitted same-sex marriage until the Massachusetts Supreme Judicial Court held in 2003 that limiting marriage to opposite-sex couples violated the State Constitution. Nor is the right to same-sex marriage deeply rooted in the traditions of other nations. No country allowed same-sex couples to marry until the Netherlands did so in 2000.

What Windsor and the United States seek, therefore, is not the protection of a deeply rooted right but the recognition of a very new right, and they seek this innovation not from a legislative body elected by the people, but from unelected judges. Faced with such a request, judges have cause for both caution and humility.

The family is an ancient and universal human institution. Family structure reflects the characteristics of a civilization, and changes in family structure and in the popular understanding of marriage and the family can have profound effects. Past changes in the understanding of marriage—for example, the gradual ascendance of the idea that romantic love is a prerequisite to marriage—have had far-reaching consequences. But the process by which such consequences come about is complex, involving the interaction of numerous factors, and tends to occur over an extended period of time.

We can expect something similar to take place if same-sex marriage becomes widely accepted. The long-term consequences of this change are not now known and are unlikely to be ascertainable for some time to come. There are those who think that allowing same-sex marriage will seriously undermine the institution of marriage. Others think that recognition of same-sex marriage will fortify a now-shaky institution.

At present, no one—including social scientists, philosophers, and historians—can predict with any certainty what the long-term ramifications of widespread acceptance of same-sex marriage will be. And judges are certainly not equipped to make such an assessment. The Members of this Court have the authority and the responsibility to interpret and apply the Constitution. Thus, if the Constitution contained a provision guaranteeing the right to marry a person of the same sex, it would be our duty to enforce that right. But the Constitution simply does not speak to the issue of same-sex marriage. In our system of government, ultimate sovereignty rests with the people, and the people have the right to control their own destiny. Any change on a question so fundamental should be made by the people through their elected officials.

III

Perhaps because they cannot show that same-sex marriage is a fundamental right under our Constitution, Windsor and the United States couch their arguments in equal protection terms. They argue that §3 of DOMA discriminates on the basis of sexual orientation, that classifications based on sexual orientation should trigger a form of "heightened" scrutiny, and that §3 cannot survive such scrutiny. They further maintain that the governmental interests that §3 purports to serve are not sufficiently important and that it has not been adequately shown that §3 serves those interests very well. The Court's holding, too, seems to rest on "the equal protection guarantee of the Fourteenth Amendment," although the Court is careful not to adopt most of Windsor's and the United States' argument. In my view, the approach that Windsor and the United States advocate is misguided. Our equal protection framework, upon which Windsor and the United States rely, is a judicial construct that provides a useful mechanism for analyzing a certain universe of equal protection cases. But that framework is ill suited for use in evaluating the constitutionality of laws based on the traditional understanding of marriage, which fundamentally turn on what marriage is.

Underlying our equal protection jurisprudence is the central notion that "[a] classification 'must be reasonable, not arbitrary, and must rest upon some ground of difference having a fair and substantial relation to the object of the legislation, so that all persons similarly circumstanced shall be treated alike.'" *Reed v. Reed* (1971). The modern tiers of scrutiny—on which Windsor and the United States rely so heavily—are a heuristic to help judges determine when classifications have that "fair and substantial relation to the object of the legislation." *Reed.*

So, for example, those classifications subject to strict scrutiny—*i.e.,* classifications that must be "narrowly tailored" to achieve a "compelling" government interest, *Parents Involved in Community Schools v. Seattle School Dist. No. 1* (2007)—are those that are "so seldom relevant to the achievement of any legitimate state interest that laws grounded in such considerations are deemed to reflect prejudice and antipathy." *Cleburne v. Cleburne Living Center, Inc.* (1985).

In contrast, those characteristics subject to so-called intermediate scrutiny—*i.e.,* those classifications that must be "'substantially related'" to the achievement of "important governmental objective[s]," *United States v. Virginia* (1996)—are those that are *sometimes* relevant considerations to be taken into account by legislators, but "generally provid[e] no sensible ground for different treatment," *Cleburne*. For example, the Court has held that statutory rape laws that criminalize sexual intercourse with a woman under the age of 18 years, but place no similar liability on partners of underage men, are grounded in the very real distinction that "young men and young women are not similarly situated with respect to the problems and the risks of sexual intercourse." *Michael M. v. Superior Court, Sonoma Cty.* (1981) (plurality opinion). The plurality reasoned that "[o]nly women may become pregnant, and they suffer disproportionately the profound physical, emotional, and psychological consequences of sexual activity." In other contexts, however, the Court has found that classifications based on gender are "arbitrary," and based on "outmoded notions of the relative capabilities of men and women," *Cleburne,* as when a State provides that a man must always be preferred to an equally qualified woman when both seek to administer the estate of a deceased party.

Finally, so-called rational-basis review applies to classifications based on "distinguishing characteristics relevant to interests the State has the authority to implement." *Cleburne*. We have long recognized that "the equal protection of the laws must coexist with the practical necessity that most legislation classifies for one purpose or another, with resulting disadvantages to various groups or persons." *Romer v. Evans* (1996). As a result, in rational-basis cases, where the court does not view the classification at issue as "inherently suspect," *Adarand Constructors, Inc. v. Peña* (1995), "the courts have been very reluctant, as they should be in our federal system and with our respect for the separation of powers, to closely scrutinize legislative choices as to whether, how, and to what extent those interests should be pursued." *Cleburne*.

In asking the Court to determine that §3 of DOMA is subject to and violates heightened scrutiny, Windsor and the United States thus ask us to rule that the presence of two members of the opposite sex is as rationally related to marriage as white skin is to voting or a Y-chromosome is to the ability to administer an estate. That is a striking request and one that unelected judges should pause before granting. Acceptance of the argument would cast all those who cling to traditional beliefs about the nature of marriage in the role of bigots or superstitious fools.

By asking the Court to strike down DOMA as not satisfying some form of heightened scrutiny, Windsor and the United States are really seeking to have the Court resolve a debate between two competing views of marriage.

The first and older view, which I will call the "traditional" or "conjugal" view, sees marriage as an intrinsically opposite-sex institution. BLAG notes that virtually every culture, including many not influenced by the Abrahamic religions, has limited marriage to people of the opposite sex. And BLAG attempts to explain this phenomenon by arguing that the institution of marriage was created for the purpose of channeling heterosexual intercourse into a structure that supports child rearing. Others explain the basis for the institution in more philosophical terms. They argue that marriage is essentially the solemnizing of a comprehensive, exclusive, permanent union that is intrinsically ordered to producing new life, even if it does not always do so. While modern cultural changes have weakened the link between marriage and procreation in the popular mind, there is no doubt that, throughout human history and across many cultures, marriage has been viewed as an exclusively opposite-sex institution and as one inextricably linked to procreation and biological kinship. The other, newer view is what I will call the "consent-based" vision of marriage, a vision that primarily defines marriage as the solemnization of mutual commitment—marked by strong emotional attachment and sexual attraction—between two persons. At least as it applies to heterosexual couples, this view of marriage now plays a very prominent role in the popular understanding of the institution. Indeed, our popular culture is infused with this understanding of marriage. Proponents of same-sex marriage argue that because gender differentiation is not relevant to this vision, the exclusion of same-sex couples from the institution of marriage is rank discrimination. The Constitution does not codify either of these views of marriage (although I suspect it would have been hard at the time of the adoption of the Constitution or the Fifth Amendment to find Americans who did not take the traditional view for granted). The silence of the Constitution on this question should be enough to end the matter as far as the judiciary is concerned. Yet, Windsor and the United States implicitly ask us to endorse the consent-based view of marriage and to reject the traditional view, thereby arrogating to ourselves the power to decide a question that philosophers, historians, social scientists, and theologians are better qualified to explore. Because our constitutional order assigns the resolution of questions of this nature to the people, I would not presume to enshrine either vision of marriage in our constitutional jurisprudence.

Legislatures, however, have little choice but to decide between the two views. We have long made clear that neither the political branches of the Federal Government nor state governments are required to be neutral between competing visions of the good, provided that the vision of the good that they adopt is not countermanded by the Constitution. Accordingly, both Congress and the States are entitled to enact laws recognizing either of the two understandings of marriage. And given the size of government and the degree to which it now regulates daily life, it seems unlikely that either Congress or the States could maintain complete neutrality even if they tried assiduously to do so.

Rather than fully embracing the arguments made by Windsor and the United States, the Court strikes down §3 of DOMA as a classification not properly supported by its objectives. The Court reaches this conclusion in part because it believes that §3 encroaches upon the States' sovereign prerogative to define marriage. Indeed, the Court's ultimate conclusion is that DOMA falls afoul of the Fifth Amendment because it "singles out a class of persons deemed *by a State* entitled to recognition and protection to enhance their own liberty" and "imposes a disability on the class by refusing to acknowledge a status *the State finds* to be dignified and proper." (emphasis added).

To the extent that the Court takes the position that the question of same-sex marriage should be resolved primarily at the state level, I wholeheartedly agree.

I hope that the Court will ultimately permit the people of each State to decide this question for themselves. Unless the Court is willing to allow this to occur, the whiffs of federalism in the today's opinion of the Court will soon be scattered to the wind.

In any event, §3 of DOMA, in my view, does not encroach on the prerogatives of the States, assuming of course that the many federal statutes affected by DOMA have not already done so. Section 3 does not prevent any State from recognizing same-sex marriage or from extending to same-sex couples any right, privilege, benefit, or obligation stemming from state law. All that §3 does is to define a class of persons to whom federal law extends certain special benefits and upon whom federal law imposes certain special burdens. In these provisions, Congress used marital status as a way of defining this class—in part, I assume, because it viewed marriage as a valuable institution to be fostered and in part because it viewed married couples as comprising a unique type of economic unit that merits special regulatory treatment. Assuming that Congress has the power under the Constitution to enact the laws affected by §3, Congress has the power to define the category of persons to whom those laws apply.

* * *

For these reasons, I would hold that §3 of DOMA does not violate the Fifth Amendment. I respectfully dissent.

# *Chapter 6*

# *Taking Private Property for Public Use*

## *ASSIGNMENT S-7*

## What Is a "Taking"?

*STUDY GUIDE:*

- Do you agree with Justice Kagan that *Nollan* and *Dolan* do not apply here because no taking of private property has occurred? What is her theory of those two cases?
- Hasn't the government agency simply failed to allow a particular use of property rather than "taken" it?
- What work is the concept of "unconstitutional conditions" (and the First Amendment cases cited) doing in Justice Alito's analysis? What is the evil he seeks to prevent? Are you persuaded by Justice Kagan's reply to this?
- Why the discussion of taxes? (For that matter, why aren't taxes "takings"?)
- Put another way, could there be a difference between a "tax" and (in Justice Kagan's words) "requiring a person to pay money to the government, or spend money on its behalf"? Does her treatment of liens suggest a possible way to distinguish a "tax" from the monetary fee the government is charging here for the use of private property?
- Notice that the property owner requested permission to build in 1994, and this case is now being remanded for further consideration by the lower courts. How effective is this constitutional protection of private property?

### KOONTZ v. ST. JOHNS RIVER WATER MANAGEMENT DISTRICT

*No. 11-1447. | Decided June 25, 2013*

ALITO, J., delivered the opinion of the Court, in which ROBERTS, C.J., and SCALIA, KENNEDY, and THOMAS, JJ., joined. KAGAN, J., filed a dissenting opinion, in which GINSBURG, BREYER, and SOTOMAYOR, JJ., joined.

JUSTICE ALITO delivered the opinion of the Court.

Our decisions in *Nollan v. California Coastal Comm'n* (1987), and *Dolan v. City of Tigard* (1994), provide important protection against the misuse of the power of land-use regulation. In those cases, we held that a unit of government may not condition the approval of a land-use permit on the owner's relinquishment of a portion of his property unless there is a "nexus" and "rough proportionality" between the government's demand and the effects of the proposed land use. In this case, the St. Johns River Water Management District (District) believes that it circumvented *Nollan* and *Dolan* because of the way in which it structured its handling of a permit application submitted by Coy Koontz, Sr., whose estate is represented in this Court by Coy Koontz, Jr. The District did not approve his application on the condition that he surrender an interest in his land. Instead, the District, after suggesting that he could obtain approval by signing over such an interest, denied his application because he refused to yield. The Florida Supreme Court blessed this maneuver and thus effectively interred those important decisions. Because we conclude that *Nollan* and *Dolan* cannot be evaded in this way, the Florida Supreme Court's decision must be reversed.

## I

### A

In 1972, petitioner purchased an undeveloped 14.9-acre tract of land on the south side of Florida State Road 50, a divided four-lane highway east of Orlando. The property is located less than 1,000 feet from that road's intersection with Florida State Road 408, a tolled expressway that is one of Orlando's major thoroughfares.

A drainage ditch runs along the property's western edge, and high-voltage power lines bisect it into northern and southern sections. The combined effect of the ditch, a 100-foot wide area kept clear for the power lines, the highways, and other construction on nearby parcels is to isolate the northern section of petitioner's property from any other undeveloped land. Although largely classified as wetlands by the State, the northern section drains well; the most significant standing water forms in ruts in an unpaved road used to access the power lines. The natural topography of the property's southern section is somewhat more diverse, with a small creek, forested uplands, and wetlands that sometimes have water as much as a foot deep. A wildlife survey found evidence of animals that often frequent developed areas: raccoons, rabbits, several species of bird, and a turtle. The record also indicates that the land may be a suitable habitat for opossums.

The same year that petitioner purchased his property, Florida enacted the Water Resources Act, which divided the State into five water management districts and authorized each district to regulate "construction that connects to, draws water from, drains water into, or is placed in or across the waters in the state." Under the Act, a landowner wishing to undertake such construction must obtain from the relevant district a Management and Storage of Surface Water (MSSW) permit, which may impose "such reasonable conditions" on the permit as are "necessary to assure" that construction will "not be harmful to the water resources of the district."

In 1984, in an effort to protect the State's rapidly diminishing wetlands, the Florida Legislature passed the Warren S. Henderson Wetlands Protection Act, which made it illegal for anyone to "dredge or fill in, on, or over surface waters" without a Wetlands Resource Management (WRM) permit. Under the Henderson Act, permit applicants are required to provide "reasonable assurance" that proposed construction on wetlands is "not contrary to the public interest," as defined by an enumerated list of criteria. Consistent with the Henderson Act, the St. Johns River Water Management District, the district with jurisdiction over petitioner's land, requires that permit applicants wishing to build on wetlands offset the resulting environmental damage by creating, enhancing, or preserving wetlands elsewhere.

Petitioner decided to develop the 3.7-acre northern section of his property, and in 1994 he applied to the District for MSSW and WRM permits. Under his proposal, petitioner would have raised the elevation of the northernmost section of his land to make it suitable for a building, graded the land from the southern edge of the building site down to the elevation of the high-voltage electrical lines, and installed a dry-bed pond for retaining and gradually releasing stormwater runoff from the building and its parking lot. To mitigate the environmental effects of his proposal, petitioner offered to foreclose any possible future development of the approximately 11-acre southern section of his land by deeding to the District a conservation easement on that portion of his property.

The District considered the 11-acre conservation easement to be inadequate, and it informed petitioner that it would approve construction only if he agreed to one of two concessions. First, the District proposed that petitioner reduce the size of his development to 1 acre and deed to the District a conservation easement on the remaining 13.9 acres. To reduce the development area, the District suggested that petitioner could eliminate the dry-bed pond from his proposal and instead install a more costly subsurface stormwater management system beneath the building site. The District also suggested that petitioner install retaining walls rather than gradually sloping the land from the building site down to the elevation of the rest of his property to the south.

In the alternative, the District told petitioner that he could proceed with the development as proposed, building on 3.7 acres and deeding a conservation easement to the government on the remainder of the property, if he also agreed to hire contractors to make improvements to District-owned land several miles away. Specifically, petitioner could pay to replace culverts on one parcel or fill in ditches on another. Either of those projects would have enhanced approximately 50 acres of District-owned wetlands. When the District asks permit applicants to fund offsite mitigation work, its policy is never to require any particular offsite project, and it did not do so here. Instead, the District said that it "would also favorably consider" alternatives to its suggested offsite mitigation projects if petitioner proposed something "equivalent."

Believing the District's demands for mitigation to be excessive in light of the environmental effects that his building proposal would have caused, petitioner filed suit in state court. Among other claims, he argued that he was entitled to relief under Fla. Stat. §373.617(2), which allows owners to recover "monetary damages" if a state agency's action is "an unreasonable exercise of the state's police power constituting a taking without just compensation."

B

The Florida Circuit Court . . . held a 2–day bench trial. After considering testimony from several experts who examined petitioner's property, the trial court found that the property's northern section had already been "seriously degraded" by extensive construction on the surrounding parcels. In light of this finding and petitioner's offer to dedicate nearly three-quarters of his land to the District, the trial court concluded that any further mitigation in the form of payment for offsite improvements to District property lacked both a nexus and rough proportionality to the environmental impact of the proposed construction. It accordingly held the District's actions unlawful under our decisions in *Nollan* and *Dolan.*

The Florida District Court [of Appeals] affirmed, but the State Supreme Court reversed. A majority of that court distinguished *Nollan* and *Dolan* on two grounds. First, the majority thought it significant that in this case, unlike *Nollan* or *Dolan,* the District did not approve petitioner's application on the condition that he accede to the District's demands; instead, the District denied his application because he refused to make concessions. Second, the majority drew a distinction between a demand for an interest in real property (what happened in *Nollan* and *Dolan*) and a demand for money. . . .

Recognizing that the majority opinion rested on a question of federal constitutional law on which the lower courts are divided, we granted the petition for a writ of certiorari, and now reverse.

II

A

We have said in a variety of contexts that "the government may not deny a benefit to a person because he exercises a constitutional right." *Regan v. Taxation With Representation of Wash.* (1983). In *Perry v. Sindermann* (1972), for example, we held that a public college would violate a professor's freedom of speech if it declined to renew his contract because he was an outspoken critic of the college's administration. And in *Memorial Hospital v. Maricopa County* (1974), we concluded that a county impermissibly burdened the right to travel by extending healthcare benefits only to those indigent sick who had been residents of the county for at least one year. Those cases reflect an overarching principle, known as the unconstitutional conditions doctrine, that vindicates the Constitution's enumerated rights by preventing the government from coercing people into giving them up.

*Nollan* and *Dolan* "involve a special application" of this doctrine that protects the Fifth Amendment right to just compensation for property the government takes when owners apply for land-use permits. *Lingle v. Chevron U.S.A. Inc.* (2005). Our decisions in those cases reflect two realities of the permitting process. The first is that land-use permit applicants are especially vulnerable to the type of coercion that the unconstitutional conditions doctrine prohibits because the government often has broad discretion to deny a permit that is worth far more than property it would like to take. By conditioning a building permit on the owner's deeding over a public right-of-way, for example, the government can pressure an owner into voluntarily giving up property for which the Fifth Amendment would otherwise require just compensation. So long as the building permit is more valuable than any just compensation the owner could hope to receive for the right-of-way, the owner is likely to accede to the government's demand, no matter how unreasonable. Extortionate demands of this sort frustrate the Fifth Amendment right to just compensation, and the unconstitutional conditions doctrine prohibits them.

A second reality of the permitting process is that many proposed land uses threaten to impose costs on the public that dedications of property can offset. Where a building proposal would substantially increase traffic congestion, for example, officials might condition permit approval on the owner's agreement to deed over the land needed to widen a public road. Respondent argues that a similar rationale justifies the exaction at issue here: petitioner's proposed construction project, it submits, would destroy wetlands on his property, and in order to compensate for this loss, respondent demands that he enhance wetlands elsewhere. Insisting that landowners internalize the negative externalities of their conduct is a hallmark of responsible land-use policy, and we have long sustained such regulations against constitutional attack. See *Village of Euclid v. Ambler Realty Co.* (1926).

*Nollan* and *Dolan* accommodate both realities by allowing the government to condition approval of a permit on the dedication of property to the public so long as there is a "nexus" and "rough proportionality" between the property that the government demands and the social costs of the applicant's proposal. Our precedents thus enable permitting authorities to insist that applicants bear the full costs of their proposals while still forbidding the government from engaging in "out-and-out . . . extortion" that would thwart the Fifth Amendment right to just compensation. Under *Nollan* and *Dolan* the government may choose whether and how a permit applicant is required to mitigate the impacts of a proposed development, but it may not leverage its legitimate interest in mitigation to pursue governmental ends that lack an essential nexus and rough proportionality to those impacts.

### B

The principles that undergird our decisions in *Nollan* and *Dolan* do not change depending on whether the government *approves* a permit on the condition that the applicant turn over property or *denies* a permit because the applicant refuses to do so. We have often concluded that denials of governmental benefits were impermissible under the unconstitutional conditions doctrine. See, *e.g., Perry* (explaining that the government "*may not deny* a benefit to a person on a basis that infringes his constitutionally protected interests" (emphasis added)). In so holding, we have recognized that regardless of whether the government ultimately succeeds in pressuring someone into forfeiting a constitutional right, the unconstitutional conditions doctrine forbids burdening the Constitution's enumerated rights by coercively withholding benefits from those who exercise them.

A contrary rule would be especially untenable in this case because it would enable the government to evade the limitations of *Nollan* and *Dolan* simply by phrasing its demands for property as conditions precedent to permit approval. Under the Florida Supreme Court's approach, a government order stating that a permit is "approved if" the owner turns over property would be subject to *Nollan* and *Dolan,* but an identical order that uses the words "denied until" would not. Our unconstitutional conditions cases have long refused to attach significance to the distinction between conditions precedent and conditions subsequent. To do so here would effectively render *Nollan* and *Dolan* a dead letter.

The Florida Supreme Court puzzled over how the government's demand for property can violate the Takings Clause even though "no property of any kind was ever taken," but the unconstitutional conditions doctrine provides a ready answer. Extortionate demands for property in the land-use permitting context run afoul of the Takings Clause not because they take property but because they impermissibly burden the right not to have property taken without just compensation. As in other unconstitutional conditions cases in which someone refuses to cede a constitutional right in the face of coercive pressure, the impermissible denial of a governmental benefit is a constitutionally cognizable injury.

Nor does it make a difference, as respondent suggests, that the government might have been able to deny petitioner's application outright without giving him the option of securing a permit by agreeing to spend money to improve public lands. Virtually all of our unconstitutional conditions cases involve a gratuitous governmental benefit of some kind. Yet we have repeatedly rejected the argument that if the government need not confer a benefit at all, it can withhold the benefit because someone refuses to give up constitutional rights. *E.g., United States v. American Library Assn., Inc.* (2003) ("[T]he government may not deny a benefit to a person on a basis that infringes his constitutionally protected . . . freedom of speech *even if he has no entitlement to that benefit*"); *Wieman v. Updegraff* (1952) (explaining in unconstitutional conditions case that to focus on "the facile generalization that there is no constitutionally protected right to public employment is to obscure the issue"). Even if respondent would have been entirely within its rights in denying the permit for some other reason, that greater authority does not imply a lesser power to condition permit approval on petitioner's forfeiture of his constitutional rights. See *Nollan* (explaining that "[t]he evident constitutional propriety" of prohibiting a land use "disappears . . . if the condition substituted for the prohibition utterly fails to further the end advanced as the justification for the prohibition"). . . .

C

. . . [R]espondent argues that we need not decide whether its demand for off-site improvements satisfied *Nollan* and *Dolan* because it gave petitioner another avenue for obtaining permit approval. Specifically, respondent said that it would have approved a revised permit application that reduced the footprint of petitioner's proposed construction site from 3.7 acres to 1 acre and placed a conservation easement on the remaining 13.9 acres of petitioner's land. Respondent argues that regardless of whether its demands for offsite mitigation satisfied *Nollan* and *Dolan,* we must separately consider each of petitioner's options, one of which did not require any of the offsite work the trial court found objectionable.

Respondent's argument is flawed because the option to which it points—developing only 1 acre of the site and granting a conservation easement on the rest—involves the same issue as the option to build on 3.7 acres and perform offsite mitigation. We agree with respondent that, so long as a permitting authority offers the landowner at least one alternative that would satisfy *Nollan* and *Dolan,* the landowner has not been subjected to an unconstitutional condition. But respondent's suggestion that we should treat its offer to let petitioner build on 1 acre as an alternative to offsite mitigation misapprehends the governmental benefit that petitioner was denied. Petitioner sought to develop 3.7 acres, but respondent in effect told petitioner that it would not allow him to build on 2.7 of those acres unless he agreed to spend money improving public lands. Petitioner claims that he was wrongfully denied a permit to build on those 2.7 acres. For that reason, respondent's offer to approve a less ambitious building project does not obviate the need to determine whether the demand for offsite mitigation satisfied *Nollan* and *Dolan.*

### III

We turn to the Florida Supreme Court's alternative holding that petitioner's claim fails because respondent asked him to spend money rather than give up an easement on his land. A predicate for any unconstitutional conditions claim is that the government could not have constitutionally ordered the person asserting the claim to do what it attempted to pressure that person into doing. For that reason, we began our analysis in both *Nollan* and *Dolan* by observing that if the government had directly seized the easements it sought to obtain through the permitting process, it would have committed a *per se* taking. The Florida Supreme Court held that petitioner's claim fails at this first step because the subject of the exaction at issue here was money rather than a more tangible interest in real property. Respondent and the dissent take the same position, citing the concurring and dissenting opinions in *Eastern Enterprises v. Apfel* (1998) for the proposition that an obligation to spend money can never provide the basis for a takings claim.

We note as an initial matter that if we accepted this argument it would be very easy for land-use permitting officials to evade the limitations of *Nollan* and *Dolan*. Because the government need only provide a permit applicant with one alternative that satisfies the nexus and rough proportionality standards, a permitting authority wishing to exact an easement could simply give the owner a choice of either surrendering an easement or making a payment equal to the easement's value. Such so-called "in lieu of" fees are utterly commonplace, and they are functionally equivalent to other types of land use exactions. For that reason and those that follow, we reject respondent's argument and hold that so-called "monetary exactions" must satisfy the nexus and rough proportionality requirements of *Nollan* and *Dolan*.

A

In *Eastern Enterprises,* the United States retroactively imposed on a former mining company an obligation to pay for the medical benefits of retired miners and their families. A four-Justice plurality concluded that the statute's imposition of retroactive financial liability was so arbitrary that it violated the Takings Clause. Although Justice Kennedy concurred in the result on due process grounds, he joined four other Justices in dissent in arguing that the Takings Clause does not apply to government-imposed financial obligations that "d[o] not operate upon or alter an identified property interest." Relying on the concurrence and dissent in *Eastern Enterprises,* respondent argues that a requirement that petitioner spend money improving public lands could not give rise to a taking.

Respondent's argument rests on a mistaken premise. Unlike the financial obligation in *Eastern Enterprises,* the demand for money at issue here did "operate upon . . . an identified property interest" by directing the owner of a particular piece of property to make a monetary payment. In this case, unlike *Eastern Enterprises,* the monetary obligation burdened petitioner's ownership of a specific parcel of land. In that sense, this case bears resemblance to our cases holding that the government must pay just compensation when it takes a lien—a right to receive money that is secured by a particular piece of property. The fulcrum this case turns on is the direct link between the government's demand and a specific parcel of real property.[1] Because of that direct link, this case implicates the central concern of *Nollan* and *Dolan*: the risk that the government may use its substantial power and discretion in land-use permitting to pursue governmental ends that lack an essential nexus and rough proportionality to the effects of the proposed new use of the specific property at issue, thereby diminishing without justification the value of the property. . . .

B

Respondent and the dissent argue that if monetary exactions are made subject to scrutiny under *Nollan* and *Dolan,* then there will be no principled way of distinguishing impermissible land-use exactions from property taxes. We think they exaggerate both the extent to which that problem is unique to the land-

1. Thus, because the proposed offsite mitigation obligation in this case was tied to a particular parcel of land, this case does not implicate the question whether monetary exactions must be tied to a particular parcel of land in order to constitute a taking. That is so even when the demand is considered "outside the permitting process." The unconstitutional conditions analysis requires us to set aside petitioner's permit application, not his ownership of a particular parcel of real property.

use permitting context and the practical difficulty of distinguishing between the power to tax and the power to take by eminent domain.

It is beyond dispute that "[t]axes and user fees . . . are not 'takings.'" [*Brown v. Legal Foundation of Wash.* (2003)] (Scalia, J., dissenting). . . . This case therefore does not affect the ability of governments to impose property taxes, user fees, and similar laws and regulations that may impose financial burdens on property owners.

At the same time, we have repeatedly found takings where the government, by confiscating financial obligations, achieved a result that could have been obtained by imposing a tax. Most recently, in *Brown,* we were unanimous in concluding that a State Supreme Court's seizure of the interest on client funds held in escrow was a taking despite the unquestionable constitutional propriety of a tax that would have raised exactly the same revenue. . . . Perhaps most closely analogous to the present case, we have repeatedly held that the government takes property when it seizes liens, and in so ruling we have never considered whether the government could have achieved an economically equivalent result through taxation.

Two facts emerge from those cases. The first is that the need to distinguish taxes from takings is not a creature of our holding today that monetary exactions are subject to scrutiny under *Nollan* and *Dolan*. Rather, the problem is inherent in this Court's long-settled view that property the government could constitutionally demand through its taxing power can also be taken by eminent domain.

Second, our cases show that teasing out the difference between taxes and takings is more difficult in theory than in practice. *Brown* is illustrative. Similar to respondent in this case, the respondents in *Brown* argued that extending the protections of the Takings Clause to a bank account would open a Pandora's Box of constitutional challenges to taxes. But also like respondent here, the *Brown* respondents never claimed that they were exercising their power to levy taxes when they took the petitioners' property. Any such argument would have been implausible under state law; in Washington, taxes are levied by the legislature, not the courts.

The same dynamic is at work in this case because Florida law greatly circumscribes respondent's power to tax. If respondent had argued that its demand for money was a tax, it would have effectively conceded that its denial of petitioner's permit was improper under Florida law. Far from making that concession, respondent has maintained throughout this litigation that it considered petitioner's money to be a substitute for his deeding to the public a conservation easement on a larger parcel of undeveloped land.

This case does not require us to say more. We need not decide at precisely what point a land-use permitting charge denominated by the government as a "tax" becomes "so arbitrary . . . that it was not the exertion of taxation but a confiscation of property." *Brushaber v. Union Pacific R. Co.* (1916). For present purposes, it suffices to say that despite having long recognized that "the power of taxation should not be confused with the power of eminent domain," *Houck v. Little River Drainage Dist.* (1915), we have had little trouble distinguishing between the two.

C

Finally, we disagree with the dissent's forecast that our decision will work a revolution in land use law by depriving local governments of the ability to charge reasonable permitting fees. Numerous courts—including courts in many of our Nation's most populous States—have confronted constitutional challenges to monetary exactions over the last two decades and applied the standard from *Nollan* and *Dolan* or something like it. Yet the "significant practical harm" the dissent predicts has not come to pass. That is hardly surprising, for the dissent is correct that state law normally provides an independent check on excessive land use permitting fees.

The dissent criticizes the notion that the Federal Constitution places any meaningful limits on "whether one town is overcharging for sewage, or another is setting the price to sell liquor too high." But only two pages later, it identifies three constraints on land use permitting fees that it says the Federal Constitution imposes and suggests that the additional protections of *Nollan* and *Dolan* are not needed. In any event, the dissent's argument that land use permit applicants need no further protection when the government demands money is really an argument for overruling *Nollan* and *Dolan*. After all, the Due Process Clause protected the Nollans from an unfair allocation of public burdens, and they too could have argued that the government's demand for property amounted to a taking under the *Penn Central* framework. We have repeatedly rejected the dissent's contention that other constitutional doctrines leave no room for the nexus and rough proportionality requirements of *Nollan* and *Dolan*. Mindful of the special vulnerability of land use permit applicants to extortionate demands for money, we do so again today.

* * *

We hold that the government's demand for property from a land-use permit applicant must satisfy the requirements of *Nollan* and *Dolan* even when the government denies the permit and even when its demand is for money. The Court expresses no view on the merits of petitioner's claim that respondent's actions here failed to comply with the principles set forth in this opinion and those two cases. The Florida Supreme Court's judgment is reversed, and this case is remanded for further proceedings not inconsistent with this opinion.

*It is so ordered.*

JUSTICE KAGAN, with whom JUSTICE GINSBURG, JUSTICE BREYER, and JUSTICE SOTOMAYOR join, dissenting.

In the paradigmatic case triggering review under *Nollan v. California Coastal Comm'n* (1987), and *Dolan v. City of Tigard* (1994), the government approves a building permit on the condition that the landowner relinquish an interest in real property, like an easement. . . . [T]he *Nollan–Dolan* test applies only when the property the government demands during the permitting process is the kind it otherwise would have to pay for—or, put differently, when the appropriation of that property, outside the permitting process, would constitute a taking. That is why *Nollan* began by stating that "[h]ad California simply required the Nollans to make an easement across their beachfront available to the public . . . , rather than conditioning their permit to rebuild their house on their agreeing to do so, we have no doubt there would have been a taking" requiring just compensation. And it is why *Dolan* started by maintaining that "had the city simply required petitioner to dedicate a strip of land . . . for public use, rather than conditioning the grant of her permit to [d]evelop her property on such a dedication, a taking would have occurred." Even the majority acknowledges this basic point about *Nollan* and *Dolan*: It too notes that those cases rest on the premise that "if the government had directly seized the easements it sought to obtain through the permitting process, it would have committed a *per se* taking." Only if that is true could the government's demand for the property force a landowner to relinquish his constitutional right to just compensation.

Here, Koontz claims that the District demanded that he spend money to improve public wetlands, not that he hand over a real property interest. . . . The key question then is: Independent of the permitting process, does requiring a person to pay money to the government, or spend money on its behalf, constitute a taking requiring just compensation? Only if the answer is yes does the *Nollan–Dolan* test apply.

But we have already answered that question no. *Eastern Enterprises v. Apfel*, as the Court describes, involved a federal statute requiring a former mining company to pay a large sum of money for the health benefits of retired employees. Five Members of the Court determined that the law did not effect a taking, distinguishing between the appropriation of a specific property interest and the imposition of an order to pay money. Justice Kennedy acknowledged in his controlling opinion that the statute "impose[d] a staggering financial burden" (which influenced his conclusion that it violated due process). Still, Justice Kennedy explained, the law did not effect a taking because it did not "operate upon or alter" a "specific and identified propert[y] or property right[ ]." Instead, "[t]he law simply imposes an obligation to perform an act, the payment of benefits. The statute is indifferent as to how the regulated entity elects to comply or the property it uses to do so." Justice Breyer, writing for four more Justices, agreed. He stated that the Takings Clause applies only when the government appropriates a "specific interest in physical or intellectual property" or "a specific, separately identifiable fund of money"; by contrast, the Clause has no bearing when the government imposes "an ordinary liability to pay money." (dissenting opinion).

Thus, a requirement that a person pay money to repair public wetlands is not a taking. Such an order does not affect a "specific and identified propert[y] or property right[ ]"; it simply "imposes an obligation to perform an act" (the improvement of wetlands) that costs money. *Id.* (opinion of Kennedy, J.). To be sure, when a person spends money on the government's behalf, or pays money directly to the government, it "will reduce [his] net worth"—but that "can be said of any law which has an adverse economic effect" on someone. *Id.* Because the government is merely imposing a "general liability" to pay money, *id.* (Breyer, J., dissenting)—and therefore is "indifferent as to how the regulated entity elects to comply or the property it uses to do so," *id.* (opinion of Kennedy, J.)—the order to repair wetlands, viewed independent of the permitting process, does not constitute a taking. And that means the order does not trigger the *Nollan–Dolan* test, because it does not force Koontz to relinquish a constitutional right.

The majority tries to distinguish *Apfel* by asserting that the District's demand here was "closely analogous" (and "bears resemblance") to the seizure of a lien on property or an income stream from a parcel of land. . . . But the majority's citations succeed only in showing what this casc is *not*. When the government dissolves a lien, or appropriates a determinate income stream from a piece of property—or, for that matter, seizes a particular "bank account or [the] accrued interest" on it—the government indeed takes a "specific" and "identified property interest." *Apfel* (opinion of Kennedy, J.). But nothing like that occurred here. The District did not demand any particular lien, or bank account, or income stream from property. It just ordered Koontz to spend or pay money. . . . Koontz's liability would have been the same whether his property produced income or not—*e.g.*, even if all he wanted to build was a family home. And similarly, Koontz could meet that obligation from whatever source he chose—a checking account, shares of stock, a wealthy uncle; the District was "indifferent as to how [he] elect[ed] to [pay] or the property [he] use[d] to do so." *Id.* No more than in *Apfel*, then, was the (supposed) demand here for a "specific and identified" piece of property, which the government could not take without paying for it.

The majority thus falls back on the sole way the District's alleged demand related to a property interest: The demand arose out of the permitting process for Koontz's land. But under the analytic framework that *Nollan* and *Dolan* established, that connection alone is insufficient to trigger heightened scrutiny. As I have described, the heightened standard of *Nollan* and *Dolan* is not a freestanding protection for land-use permit applicants; rather, it is "a special application of the doctrine of unconstitutional conditions, which provides that the government may not require a person to give up a constitutional right—here the right to receive just compensation when property is taken"—in exchange for a land-use permit. [*Lingle v. Chevron U.S.A. Inc.* (2005)]. As such, *Nollan* and *Dolan* apply only if the demand at issue would have violated the Constitution independent of that proposed exchange. Or put otherwise, those cases apply only if the demand would have constituted a taking when executed *outside* the permitting process. And here, under *Apfel*, it would not.[2]

2. The majority's sole response is that "the unconstitutional conditions analysis requires us to set aside petitioner's permit application, not his ownership of a particular parcel of real property." That mysterious sentence fails to make the majority's opinion cohere with the unconstitutional conditions doctrine, as anyone has ever known it. That doctrine applies only if imposing a condition directly—*i.e.*, independent of an exchange for a government benefit—would violate the Constitution. Here, *Apfel* makes clear that the District's condition would not do so: The government may (separate and apart from permitting) require a person—whether Koontz or anyone else—to pay or spend money without effecting a taking. The majority offers no theory to the contrary: It does not explain, as it must, why the District's condition was "unconstitutional."

The majority's approach, on top of its analytic flaws, threatens significant practical harm. By applying *Nollan* and *Dolan* to permit conditions requiring monetary payments—with no express limitation except as to taxes—the majority extends the Takings Clause, with its notoriously "difficult" and "perplexing" standards, into the very heart of local land-use regulation and service delivery. Cities and towns across the nation impose many kinds of permitting fees every day. Some enable a government to mitigate a new development's impact on the community, like increased traffic or pollution—or destruction of wetlands. Others cover the direct costs of providing services like sewage or water to the development. Still others are meant to limit the number of landowners who engage in a certain activity, as fees for liquor licenses do. All now must meet *Nollan* and *Dolan*'s nexus and proportionality tests. The Federal Constitution thus will decide whether one town is overcharging for sewage, or another is setting the price to sell liquor too high. And the flexibility of state and local governments to take the most routine actions to enhance their communities will diminish accordingly.

That problem becomes still worse because the majority's distinction between monetary "exactions" and taxes is so hard to apply. The majority acknowledges, as it must, that taxes are not takings. But once the majority decides that a simple demand to pay money—the sort of thing often viewed as a tax—can count as an impermissible "exaction," how is anyone to tell the two apart? The question, as Justice Breyer's opinion in *Apfel* noted, "bristles with conceptual difficulties." And practical ones, too: How to separate orders to pay money from . . . well, orders to pay money, so that a locality knows what it can (and cannot) do. State courts sometimes must confront the same question, as they enforce restrictions on localities' taxing power. And their decisions—contrary to the majority's blithe assertion, struggle to draw a coherent boundary. Because "[t]here is no set rule" by which to determine "in which category a particular" action belongs, *Eastern Diversified Properties, Inc. v. Montgomery Cty.* (Md. 1990), courts often reach opposite conclusions about classifying nearly identical fees. . . . Compare, *e.g.*, *Coulter v. Rawlins* (Wyo. 1983) (holding that a fee to enhance parks, imposed as a permit condition, was a regulatory exaction), with *Home Builders Assn. v. West Des Moines* (Iowa 2002) (rejecting *Coulter* and holding that a nearly identical fee was a tax). Nor does the majority's opinion provide any help with that issue: Perhaps its most striking feature is its refusal to say even a word about how to make the distinction that will now determine whether a given fee is subject to heightened scrutiny. . . .

At bottom, the majority's analysis seems to grow out of a yen for a prophylactic rule: Unless *Nollan* and *Dolan* apply to monetary demands, the majority worries, "land-use permitting officials" could easily "evade the limitations" on exaction of real property interests that those decisions impose. But that is a prophylaxis in search of a problem. No one has presented evidence that in the many States declining to apply heightened scrutiny to permitting fees, local officials routinely short-circuit *Nollan* and *Dolan* to extort the surrender of real property interests having no relation to a development's costs. And if officials were to impose a fee as a contrivance to take an easement (or other real property right), then a court could indeed apply *Nollan* and *Dolan*. That situation does not call for a rule extending, as the majority's does, to *all* monetary exactions. Finally, a court can use the *Penn Central* framework, the Due Process Clause, and (in many places) state law to protect against monetary demands, whether or not imposed to evade *Nollan* and *Dolan,* that simply "go[ ] too far." [*Pennsylvania Coal Co. v. Mahon* (1922)].[3]

In sum, *Nollan* and *Dolan* restrain governments from using the permitting process to do what the Takings Clause would otherwise prevent—*i.e.,* take a specific property interest without just compensation. Those cases have no application when governments impose a general financial obligation as part of the permitting process, because under *Apfel* such an action does not otherwise trigger the Takings Clause's protections. By extending *Nollan* and *Dolan*'s heightened scrutiny to a simple payment demand, the majority threatens the heartland of local land-use regulation and service delivery, at a bare minimum depriving state and local governments of "necessary predictability." *Apfel* (opinion of Kennedy, J.). That decision is unwarranted—and deeply unwise. I would keep *Nollan* and *Dolan* in their intended sphere and affirm the Florida Supreme Court. . . .

III

*Nollan* and *Dolan* are important decisions, designed to curb governments from using their power over land-use permitting to extract for free what the Takings Clause would otherwise require them to pay for. But . . . the government commits a taking only when it appropriates a specific property interest, not when it requires a person to pay or spend money. Here, the District never took or threatened such an interest; it tried to extract from Koontz solely a commitment to spend money to repair public wetlands. . . . The majority's errors here are consequential. The majority turns a broad array of local land-use regulations into federal constitutional questions. It deprives state and local governments of the flexibility they need to enhance their communities—to ensure environmentally sound and economically productive development. It places courts smack

3. Our *Penn Central* test protects against regulations that unduly burden an owner's use of his property: Unlike the *Nollan–Dolan* standard, that framework fits to a T a complaint (like Koontz's) that a permitting condition makes it inordinately expensive to develop land. And the Due Process Clause provides an additional backstop against excessive permitting fees by preventing a government from conditioning a land-use permit on a monetary requirement that is "basically arbitrary." *Eastern Enterprises v. Apfel* (1998) (Breyer, J., dissenting). My point is not, as the majority suggests, that these constraints do the same thing as *Nollan* and *Dolan*, and so make those decisions unnecessary. To the contrary, *Nollan* and *Dolan* provide developers with enhanced protection (and localities with correspondingly reduced flexibility). The question here has to do not with "overruling" those cases, but with extending them. My argument is that our prior caselaw struck the right balance: heightened scrutiny when the government uses the permitting process to demand property that the Takings Clause protects, and lesser scrutiny, but a continuing safeguard against abuse, when the government's demand is for something falling outside that Clause's scope.

in the middle of the most everyday local government activity. As those consequences play out across the country, I believe the Court will rue today's decision. I respectfully dissent.

*STUDY GUIDE:*

- The next case treats the issue of whether a taking of private property must be permanent to constitute a "taking" for purposes of the Fifth Amendment.
- Just as the previous case discussed the difference between a "taking" and a "tax," how does the Court distinguish between a "taking" and a "government interference with property"?

## *ASSIGNMENT S-8*

### ARKANSAS GAME AND FISH COMMISSION v. UNITED STATES

*No. 11-597. | Decided Dec. 4, 2012*

GINSBURG, J., delivered the opinion of the Court, in which all other Members joined, except KAGAN, J., who took no part in the consideration or decision of the case.

JUSTICE GINSBURG delivered the opinion of the Court.

Periodically from 1993 until 2000, the U.S. Army Corps of Engineers (Corps) authorized flooding that extended into the peak growing season for timber on forest land owned and managed by petitioner, Arkansas Game and Fish Commission (Commission). Cumulative in effect, the repeated flooding damaged or destroyed more than 18 million board feet of timber and disrupted the ordinary use and enjoyment of the Commission's property. The Commission sought compensation from the United States pursuant to the Fifth Amendment's instruction: "[N]or shall private property be taken for public use, without just compensation." The question presented is whether a taking may occur, within the meaning of the Takings Clause, when government-induced flood invasions, although repetitive, are temporary.

Ordinarily, this Court's decisions confirm, if government action would qualify as a taking when permanently continued, temporary actions of the same character may also qualify as a taking. In the instant case, the parties and the courts below divided on the appropriate classification of temporary flooding. Reversing the judgment of the Court of Federal Claims, which awarded compensation to the Commission, the Federal Circuit held, 2 to 1, that compensation may be sought only when flooding is "a permanent or inevitably recurring condition, rather than an inherently temporary situation." 637 F.3d 1366, 1378 (2011). We disagree and conclude that recurrent floodings, even if of finite duration, are not categorically exempt from Takings Clause liability.

I

A

The Commission owns the Dave Donaldson Black River Wildlife Management Area (Management Area or Area), which comprises 23,000 acres along both banks of the Black River in northeast Arkansas. The Management Area is forested with multiple hardwood timber species that support a variety of wildlife habitats. The Commission operates the Management Area as a wildlife and hunting preserve, and also uses it as a timber resource, conducting regular harvests of timber as part of its forest-management efforts. Three types of hardwood oak species—nuttall, overcup, and willow—account for 80 percent of the trees in the Management Area. The presence of these hardwood oaks is essential to the Area's character as a habitat for migratory birds and as a venue for recreation and hunting.

The Clearwater Dam (Dam) is located 115 miles upstream from the Management Area. The Corps constructed the Dam in 1948, and shortly thereafter adopted a plan known as the Water Control Manual (Manual) to determine the rates at which water would be released from the Dam. The Manual sets seasonally varying release rates, but permits planned deviations from the prescribed rates for agricultural, recreational, and other purposes.

In 1993, the Corps approved a planned deviation in response to requests from farmers. From September to December 1993, the Corps released water from the Dam at a slower rate than usual, providing downstream farmers with a longer harvest time. As a result, more water than usual accumulated in Clearwater Lake behind the Dam. To reduce the accumulation, the Corps extended the period in which a high amount of water would be released. The Commission maintained this extension yielded downstream flooding in the Management Area, above historical norms, during the tree-growing season, which runs from April to October. If the Corps had released the water more rapidly in the fall of 1993, in accordance with the Manual and with past practice, there would have been short-term waves of flooding which would have receded quickly. The lower rate of release in the fall, however, extended the period of flooding well into the following spring and summer. While the deviation benefited farmers, it interfered with the Management Area's tree-growing season.

The Corps adopted similar deviations each year from 1994 through 2000. The record indicates that the decision to deviate from the Manual was made independently in each year and that the amount of deviation varied over the span of years. Nevertheless, the result was an unbroken string of annual deviations from the Manual. Each deviation lowered the rate at which water was released during the fall, which necessitated extension of the release period into the following spring and summer. During this span of years the Corps proposed Manual revisions that would have made its temporary deviations part of the permanent water-release plan. On multiple occasions between 1993 and 2000, the Commission objected to the temporary deviations and opposed any permanent revision to the Manual, on the ground that the departures from the traditional water-release plan adversely impacted the Management Area. Ultimately, the

Corps tested the effect of the deviations on the Management Area. It thereupon abandoned the proposal to permanently revise the Manual and, in 2001, ceased its temporary deviations.

B

In 2005, the Commission filed the instant lawsuit against the United States, claiming that the temporary deviations from the Manual constituted a taking of property that entitled the Commission to compensation. The Commission maintained that the deviations caused sustained flooding of its land during the tree-growing season. The cumulative impact of this flooding over a six-year period between 1993 and 1999, the Commission alleged, resulted in the destruction of timber in the Management Area and a substantial change in the character of the terrain, which necessitated costly reclamation measures. Following a trial, the Court of Federal Claims ruled in favor of the Commission and issued an opinion and order containing detailed findings of fact.

The Court of Federal Claims found that the forests in the Management Area were healthy and flourishing before the flooding that occurred in the 1990's, and that the forests had been sustainably managed for decades under the water-release plan contained in the Manual. It further found that the Commission repeatedly objected to the deviations from the Manual and alerted the Corps to the detrimental effect the longer period of flooding would have on the hardwood timber in the Management Area.

As found by the Court of Federal Claims, the flooding caused by the deviations contrasted markedly with historical flooding patterns. Between 1949 and 1992, the river level near the Management Area reached six feet an average of 64.7 days per year during the growing season; the number of such days had been even lower on average before the Clearwater Dam was built. Between 1993 and 1999, however, the river reached the same level an average of 91.14 days per year, an increase of more than 40 percent over the historic average. Although the Management Area lies in a floodplain, in no previously recorded time span did comparable flooding patterns occur. Evidence at trial indicated that half of the nuttall oaks in the Management Area were saturated with water when the river level was at six feet; the evidence further indicated that the saturation of the soil around the trees' root systems could persist for weeks even after the flooding had receded.

The court concluded that the Corps' deviations caused six consecutive years of substantially increased flooding, which constituted an appropriation of the Commission's property, albeit a temporary rather than a permanent one. Important to this conclusion, the court emphasized the deviations' cumulative effect. The trees were subject to prolonged periods of flooding year after year, which reduced the oxygen level in the soil and considerably weakened the trees' root systems. The repeated annual flooding for six years altered the character of the property to a much greater extent than would have been shown if the harm caused by one year of flooding were simply multiplied by six. When a moderate drought occurred in 1999 and 2000, the trees did not have the root systems necessary to sustain themselves; the result, in the court's words, was "catastrophic mortality." More than 18 million board feet of timber were destroyed or degraded.

This damage altered the character of the Management Area. The destruction of the trees led to the invasion of undesirable plant species, making natural regeneration of the forests improbable in the absence of reclamation efforts. To determine the measure of just compensation, the Court of Federal Claims calculated the value of the lost timber and the projected cost of the reclamation and awarded the Commission $5.7 million.

The Federal Circuit reversed. It acknowledged that in general, temporary government action may give rise to a takings claim if permanent action of the same character would constitute a taking. But it held that "cases involving flooding and [flowage] easements are different." Government-induced flooding can give rise to a taking claim, the Federal Circuit concluded, only if the flooding is "permanent or inevitably recurring." . . . We granted certiorari to resolve the question whether government actions that cause repeated floodings must be permanent or inevitably recurring to constitute a taking of property.

II

The Takings Clause is "designed to bar Government from forcing some people alone to bear public burdens which, in all fairness and justice, should be borne by the public as a whole." *Armstrong v. United States* (1960). And "[w]hen the government physically takes possession of an interest in property for some public purpose, it has a categorical duty to compensate the former owner." *Tahoe–Sierra Preservation Council, Inc. v. Tahoe Regional Planning Agency* (1951)). These guides are fundamental in our Takings Clause jurisprudence. We have recognized, however, that no magic formula enables a court to judge, in every case, whether a given government interference with property is a taking. In view of the nearly infinite variety of ways in which government actions or regulations can affect property interests, the Court has recognized few invariable rules in this area.

True, we have drawn some bright lines, notably, the rule that a permanent physical occupation of property authorized by government is a taking. *Loretto v. Teleprompter Manhattan CATV Corp.* (1982). So, too, is a regulation that permanently requires a property owner to sacrifice all economically beneficial uses of his or her land. *Lucas v. South Carolina Coastal Council* (1992). But aside from the cases attended by rules of this order, most takings claims turn on situation-specific factual inquiries. With this in mind, we turn to the question presented here—whether temporary flooding can ever give rise to a takings claim.

The Court first ruled that government-induced flooding can constitute a taking in *Pumpelly v. Green Bay Co.* (1872). . . . [T]he Court held that "where real estate is actually invaded by superinduced additions of water, earth, sand, or other material . . . so as to effectually destroy or impair its usefulness, it is a taking, within the meaning of the Constitution." Following *Pumpelly,* the Court recognized that seasonally recurring flooding could constitute a taking. . . .

Furthermore, our decisions confirm that takings temporary in duration can be compensable. This principle was solidly established in the World War II era, when "[c]ondemnation for indefinite periods of occupancy [took hold as] a practical response to the uncertainties of the Government's needs in wartime." *United States v. Westinghouse Elec. & Mfg. Co.* (1950). In support of the war effort, the Government took temporary possession of many properties. These exercises of government authority, the Court recognized, qualified as compensable temporary takings. Notably in relation to the question before us, the takings claims approved in these cases were not confined to instances in which the Government took outright physical possession of the property involved. A temporary takings claim could be maintained as well when government action occurring outside the property gave rise to "a direct and immediate interference with the enjoyment and use of the land." *United States v. Causby* (1946) (frequent overflights from a nearby airport resulted in a taking, for the flights deprived the property owner of the customary use of his property as a chicken farm).

Ever since, we have rejected the argument that government action must be permanent to qualify as a taking. Once the government's actions have worked a taking of property, "no subsequent action by the government can relieve it of the duty to provide compensation for the period during which the taking was effective." [*First English Evangelical Lutheran Church of Glendale v. County of Los Angeles* (1987)].

Because government-induced flooding can constitute a taking of property, and because a taking need not be permanent to be compensable, our precedent indicates that government-induced flooding of limited duration may be compensable. No decision of this Court authorizes a blanket temporary-flooding exception to our Takings Clause jurisprudence, and we decline to create such an exception in this case.

III

. . . There is . . . no solid grounding in precedent for setting flooding apart from all other government intrusions on property. And the Government has presented no other persuasive reason to do so. Its primary argument is of the in for a penny, in for a pound genre: reversing the decision below, the Government worries, risks disruption of public works dedicated to flood control. "[E]very passing flood attributable to the government's operation of a flood-control project, no matter how brief," the Government hypothesizes, might qualify as a compensable taking. To reject a categorical bar to temporary-flooding takings claims, however, is scarcely to credit all, or even many, such claims. It is of course incumbent on courts to weigh carefully the relevant factors and circumstances in each case, as instructed by our decisions.

The slippery slope argument, we note, is hardly novel or unique to flooding cases. Time and again in Takings Clause cases, the Court has heard the prophecy that recognizing a just compensation claim would unduly impede the government's ability to act in the public interest. We have rejected this argument when deployed to urge blanket exemptions from the Fifth Amendment's instruction. While we recognize the importance of the public interests the Government advances in this case, we do not see them as categorically different from the interests at stake in myriad other Takings Clause cases. . . .

IV

We rule today, simply and only, that government-induced flooding temporary in duration gains no automatic exemption from Takings Clause inspection. When regulation or temporary physical invasion by government interferes with private property, our decisions recognize, time is indeed a factor in determining the existence *vel non* of a compensable taking. Also relevant to the takings inquiry is the degree to which the invasion is intended or is the foreseeable result of authorized government action. For example, the Management Area lies in a floodplain below a dam, and had experienced flooding in the past. But the trial court found the Area had not been exposed to flooding comparable to the 1990's accumulations in any other time span either prior to or after the construction of the Dam.

The Court of Federal Claims found that the flooding the Commission assails was foreseeable. In this regard, the court noted the Commission's repeated complaints to the Corps about the destructive impact of the successive planned deviations from the Water Control Manual. Further, the court determined that the interference with the Commission's property was severe: The Commission had been deprived of the customary use of the Management Area as a forest and wildlife preserve, as the bottomland hardwood forest turned, over time, into a "headwater swamp."

The Government, however, challenged several of the trial court's factfindings, including those relating to causation, foreseeability, substantiality, and the amount of damages. Because the Federal Circuit rested its decision entirely on the temporary duration of the flooding, it did not address those challenges. As earlier noted, preserved issues remain open for consideration on remand.

* * *

For the reasons stated, the judgment of the Court of Appeals for the Federal Circuit is reversed, and the case is remanded for further proceedings consistent with this opinion.

*It is so ordered.*

JUSTICE KAGAN took no part in the consideration or decision of this case.